VISHOKA MEDITATION

ALSO BY PANDIT RAJMANI TIGUNAIT, PhD

BOOKS

The Practice of the Yoga Sutra: Sadhana Pada

The Secret of the Yoga Sutra: Samadhi Pada

The Pursuit of Power and Freedom: Katha Upanishad

Touched by Fire: The Ongoing Journey of a Spiritual Seeker

Lighting the Flame of Compassion

Inner Quest: Yoga's Answers to Life's Questions

The Himalayan Masters: A Living Tradition

Why We Fight: Practices for Lasting Peace

At the Eleventh Hour: The Biography of Swami Rama

Swami Rama of the Himalayas: His Life and Mission

Tantra Unveiled: Seducing the Forces of Matter and Spirit

Shakti: The Power in Tantra (A Scholarly Approach)

From Death to Birth: Understanding Karma and Reincarnation

The Power of Mantra and the Mystery of Initiation

Shakti Sadhana: Steps to Samadhi

Seven Systems of Indian Philosophy

AUDIO & VIDEO

Living Tantra Series DVD set

Spirit of the Vedas

Spirit of the Upanishads

Pulsation: Chants of the Maha Kumbha Mela

VISHOKA MEDITATION

The Yoga of Inner Radiance

Pandit Rajmani Tigunait, PhD

HONESDALE, PENNSYLVANIA USA

Himalayan Institute
952 Bethany Turnpike
Honesdale, PA 18431

HimalayanInstitute.org

Printed in the United States of America

23 22 21 20   2 3 4 5

ISBN-13: 978-0-89389-290-6 (paper)

Cover design and artwork by Kim Krans
Figures by Joe Kennedy

Library of Congress Control Number: 2019912603

∞ This paper meets the requirements of ANSI/NISO Z39-48-1992 (Permanence of Paper).

*In gratitude to the
Sages of the Himalayan Tradition*

Contents

Foreword

Each of us finds meditation in our own unique way. I had the good fortune to be born into a family of meditators and raised in a spiritual lineage and community in which meditation is a way of life. Looking back, I can't pinpoint when I was taught to meditate, but I do know it has become an integral part of who I am—a priceless gift that will continue to unfold for the rest of my life.

When I first read the manuscript of *Vishoka Meditation*, I saw that this book embodies the same love and guidance that my father imparted so skillfully over all these years as he taught me to meditate. He was sharing the most precious gift he received from his teachers and from the tradition they represent. This book is an embodiment of that gift.

In its fullness, meditation satisfies a fundamental human desire to be profoundly nourished and fulfilled at every level. We seek this fulfillment in our worldly experiences, yet often find they fail to provide it. Meditation helps us achieve fulfillment by introducing us to a higher reality within ourselves. Swami Rama, the founder of the Himalayan Institute, shared this essential, yet profound insight: "Meditation does that which nothing else can—it introduces you to yourself." Upon finding this inner connection, we discover the key to awakening our full human potential. This is the promise of Vishoka Meditation.

As interest in meditation has exploded in the West, an ever-expanding ecosystem of different meditation styles has emerged. In large part, these modern styles of meditation are defined by the techniques they promote and the personalities who espouse them. But accomplished meditators of the ancient past, coming from a diverse range of traditions rooted in yoga, saw meditation in a different light. To them, meditation was defined not simply by technique, but also by the body of wisdom surrounding it, and ultimately by the experience that technique evokes. This is the context in which Vishoka Meditation has arisen.

The heart of Vishoka Meditation is a technique that is spiritually grounded, yet highly systematic and experiential. As a practice, it is unique in its ability to skillfully interweave physical breath awareness with subtle pranic awareness. This engenders a concrete and increasingly deep self-awareness—one that is grounded in a tangible experience rather than in mere imagination.

But Vishoka Meditation is much more than a technique— it is a living practice supported by a rich body of experiential wisdom refined over countless generations. This wisdom feeds our practice by enabling us to understand where Vishoka Meditation comes from, why it is important, and what dynamics underpin it.

Vishoka Meditation has been lovingly stewarded and passed down by a living tradition—the Himalayan Tradition—for thousands of years. The essence of Vishoka Meditation is a unique experience of freedom from pain, coupled with inner illumination. As we practice and gain direct experience, we ourselves become living links in the tradition of Vishoka Meditation. Our practice draws support from the collective experience, love, and *sankalpa* (power of positive intention) of those who came before us. This serves as a strong foundation for our practice and a powerful catalyst for our inner growth, empowering us to share the best of ourselves with the world.

Vishoka Meditation is a gift of experiential wisdom from an ancient tradition to the modern world. Receiving wisdom and techniques grounded in the direct experience of an accomplished practitioner helps bring the practice of meditation to life so we can experience the highest promise of meditation for ourselves. This is why receiving these teachings from a living tradition is a precious gift and why this book, with the practices it offers, is the opportunity of a lifetime for modern seekers.

Ishan Tigunait

Preface

Sitting down to write this preface, I again find myself overcome by loving, tender, and nurturing memories of my first
teacher, Swami Sadananda, who guided me into the practice
of Vishoka Meditation forty-six years ago. As I wrote in the
preface to an earlier book, *The Secret of the Yoga Sutra:
Samadhi Pada*, this great soul came to my rescue when I was
drowning in a bottomless ocean of despondency and self-pity.
He imparted the distilled wisdom of his lifelong experience,
enabling me to find new meaning in everything I had
inherited from my family tradition.

He gave me the tools to process the gifts of joy and sorrow,
which often come to us intermingled. He instilled in my mind
and heart the clear understanding that good and bad, right
and wrong, pleasure and pain, success and failure, and honor
and humiliation come to us all. Most of us are shaken—
sometimes shattered—by these dichotomies. But those who are
equipped with the tools and techniques to process them remain
unperturbed and emerge victorious. In his wisdom, Swami
Sadananda showed me how a timeless text, the *Yoga Sutra*, is
the repository of such tools and techniques, and further, how
Vishoka Meditation is the most outstanding among them.

The core strength of Vishoka Meditation is that in the course of three stages of practice it gives us different sets of tools to accomplish three sets of goals. The first set of tools helps us alter the conditions that disrupt the internal ecology of our body, agitate our nervous system, dull our cognitive faculties, mute the voice of our heart, and make us fall victim to our self-defeating tendencies. When we apply these tools we acquire a clear, calm, and focused mind. By employing such a mind, we discover the root cause of our suffering and, with practice, destroy it. This results in lasting peace and happiness. We are free from fear, doubt, sorrow, regret, and self-pity— a state of consciousness known as *vishoka*.

This state of consciousness attracts the tools we need to practice the second stage of Vishoka Meditation. Practicing this stage awakens the immense power of our mind. We become deeply interested in, and capable of, envisioning and reclaiming our inner excellence. As a result, we become a fully mature human being and are inspired to explore and embrace the divinity in ourselves and in everyone else. This stage of realization attracts the tools for the third and final stage— experiencing our oneness with our creator, the Lord of Life.

I am grateful to divine providence for using me as an instrument to delineate the first stage of Vishoka Meditation here in these pages. I gratefully offer this work to the long line of masters, particularly to Patanjali, who gave us the priceless gift of the *Yoga Sutra*. I also offer my gratitude to my first teacher, Swami Sadananda, who taught me the first thirty-six sutras of this timeless text. I cherish his prophecy deep in my heart: "The thirty-sixth sutra of the *Yoga Sutra* contains the seed of Vishoka Meditation. With repeated study and contemplation, this sutra will reveal its inherent power and wisdom. One day that will result in the right understanding of Vishoka Meditation, freeing you from all forms of *shoka*, the mental tendencies that force you to remain caught in the torrent of suffering. That will also enable you to comprehend the true intent of the entire *Yoga Sutra*, *Shiva Sutra*, and *Lotus Sutra* (*Sad-Dharma Pundarika Sutra*)."

Finally, I am grateful to my master, Swami Rama, who not only guided me but also created an environment conducive to my study and practice of the *Yoga Sutra*. As I attempt to pass on the priceless gifts of all these masters, I pray that those who practice this sublime system of meditation will benefit as profoundly as I have.

VISHOKA
MEDITATION

Introduction

Vishoka Meditation is the legacy of a long line of masters who realized that transcending pain and sorrow is crucial to finding lasting happiness. For a long time this system of meditation was passed directly from teacher to student. Only when the ageless master Vyasa collected and documented a vast range of the wisdom and experiences of the past did information regarding Vishoka Meditation become available in written form. Buddha subsequently added his own personal experience and taught this system as meditation on the lotus of the heart. Three hundred years later, Patanjali, the author of the *Yoga Sutra*, elaborated on this system by using the term *vishoka*, sorrowless joy. Vishoka Meditation means "meditation on the lotus of the heart leading to sorrowless joy."

Vishoka Meditation is taught in three successive stages: first, learning how to direct the mind inward; second, discovering the wealth of our mind—*siddhis*, extraordinary powers; and third, attaining the fullness and wisdom of Sri Vidya. The first stage of the practice is designed to help us calm the nervous system, improve concentration, strengthen memory, and direct the flow of the mind inward. This inward-flowing mind is then led to discover the profound stillness at the center of our consciousness. This stage of Vishoka Meditation comprises a set of techniques that unite our mind and breath and employ these united forces to explore the previously uncharted territory of our body and mind.

This process leads us to discover our strengths and weaknesses. A mind charged with the power of breath summons its inherent wisdom and commands the body to heal and rejuvenate itself. As practice progresses, the mind may come in touch with deep-rooted emotional injuries and self-defeating mental tendencies, but unlike in the past, the inwardly flowing, empowered mind stands firm and, using its power of discernment, attenuates and eventually nullifies their negative impact. This is what masters like Buddha and Patanjali call liberation or freedom. The present volume focuses on this initial stage of Vishoka Meditation.

The secret of mastering the practice at this stage lies in the precision and effortlessness employed in uniting the mind and breath and turning their united forces inward. Mastery further depends on two things: first, adhering strictly to the sequence of techniques for uniting the mind and breath and turning them inward; and second, exercising patience. We must observe the inward movement of mind and breath at as slow a pace as possible and let the immersive state arise of its own accord. It is important to refrain from making an effort to experience tranquility and inner radiance. Instead, we let the united forces of mind and breath bring that experience forward and allow our self-awareness to bathe in it.

Beyond acquiring a peaceful mind and a relaxed nervous system, there are two major signs that we are progressing. First, preceding the main course of meditation, a non-sensory feeling of joy arises. This experience grows into a unique craving—we feel an urge to deposit this joy in the space corresponding to the center of the forehead. Second, there arises an experience of non-physical glow in that same space during the main course of the practice. This experience also grows into a unique craving—we feel an urge to sit quietly and watch the subtle pulsation of breath effortlessly moving up and down in the space corresponding to the center of the forehead. These two experiences fill us with trust in our practice and enable us to meditate without doubt, fear, or anxiety.

As our practice progresses, the brilliance and calmness of the space corresponding to the region of our forehead begin to subsume the awareness pertaining to our physical self. This is when we enter the inner space of consciousness. Experience of this inner consciousness is what is described as being here and now. This experience transcends the familiar realm of time and space and yet is as concrete as our experience of time and space in the physical world. In this space of consciousness there is no pain, no sorrow, no grief, no fear, and no doubt. Disturbances and distractions arising from the world of afflictions have no access to this space.

In the beginning, this experience may last only for a few seconds, but as the practice continues, our familiarity with this space deepens and we become increasingly drawn to it. Eventually a radical mental shift occurs—the mind loses its habit of being disturbed, distracted, and stupefied. It becomes easier for us to be peaceful than to be disturbed. We enjoy being in the present and have no concern with the past or anxiety about the future. At this point we are able to dwell in that space happily and effortlessly. This experience is the culmination of the first stage of Vishoka Meditation and the beginning of the second stage.

The second stage is characterized by our ability to bring our peaceful, joyful, and focused mind to any place in the body at will. In other words, we have a laser-focused mind. We can, for example, focus it at the center of the forehead, the heart center, or the navel center. And we can employ this highly concentrated mind to meditate on a mantra or on potent virtues, such as friendliness, compassion, love, and non-violence.

This stage is composed of techniques designed to awaken and harness the extraordinary power and wisdom of our body and mind. *Yoga nidra*; spiritual healing; clairvoyance; the ability to access the past and the future; and the ability to communicate with other creatures, including celestial beings, whose bodies are made of pure light, are a few examples of extraordinary powers associated with this second stage. In yogic literature, these abilities are called *siddhis*, and the yogis who have mastered this stage are called *siddha* masters. The first stage of Vishoka Meditation is the gateway to the second; without proficiency in the first stage, the second stage remains a mere fantasy.

The third stage is a further refinement of the second stage. The extraordinary powers gained at the second stage are now employed to unveil the mystery of consciousness and its relationship with the forces that govern our personal life and the lives of all living beings in the universe. At this stage, Vishoka evolves into mind-shattering mysticism, for it aims at nothing less than solving the mystery of birth and death and achieving immortality. The practices for casting off the body voluntarily and painlessly (*ut-kramanam*); taking on a new body at will (*parakaya pravesha*); creating a mind and body through *asmita*, pure self-awareness, without utilizing the matter and energy of the physical world; and dematerializing and meditating while using three pairs of atoms as a locus for consciousness are a few examples of the accomplishments associated with the third stage of Vishoka Meditation. All the practices belonging to this stage are part of Sri Vidya.

The first stage of Vishoka Meditation—the subject of this volume—is designed to balance the ecology of the body, restore its vitality, and make it an effective container for the mind. This initial stage is also designed to cultivate a clear, calm, and inwardly flowing mind. This process is accomplished by uniting the mind and breath. The united forces of mind and breath enable us to face and conquer our inner enemies: fear, doubt, grief, worry, anger, feelings of worthlessness, and so on. Once free of our inner turmoil, we have an opportunity to reclaim the priceless gift of divine providence—lasting peace and happiness.

This level of accomplishment inspires and empowers us to discover the infinite wealth of our own mind—siddhis, extraordinary powers. They are the hallmark of the second stage. Even a little taste fills us with enthusiasm, courage, and trust that we are destined to unveil the mystery of life and become fully connected with our creator. This realization in its own mysterious way transports us to the third stage of Vishoka, which in its fullness is known as Sri Vidya—a highly sought experience of the ancient masters.

When and how we reach stages two or three is not a question to entertain now. What matters now is that we begin practicing the first stage of Vishoka Meditation and leave the rest to providence.

CHAPTER 1

The Scope of Vishoka Meditation

Vishoka Meditation is the epitome of yogic experiences for it empowers us to face and conquer a reality we have been attempting to ignore: pain, sorrow, and fear. Pain, sorrow, and fear are always accompanied by their cure. To find this cure, we need a firm conviction and a well-polished technique. Vishoka Meditation contains both. Step by step, it guides us to transcend pain and sorrow and live without fear. It connects us to our core being, from which the healing force flows in various grades and degrees.

This meditation technique is grounded in an incontrovertible truth—the mind is the master of the body. The body acts in response to the desires, cravings, needs, and demands of the mind. When the mind is at peace, the body's limbs and organs function smoothly and harmoniously. They hear and heed the commands of the mind. The resulting experience is joy.

But when the mind is agitated, the internal ecology of the

body is disrupted and its organs and systems do not communicate with each other properly. In the absence of mutual cooperation, they function inefficiently. The resulting experience is pain. Prolonged pain and frequent bouts of pain further degrade the ecology of the body. As this vicious cycle accelerates, pain intensifies, eventually maturing into a much deeper and more potent form of pain: *shoka*—sorrow, fear, and anxiety. This potent pain—shoka—drains an enormous amount of our mental energy. The mind becomes weak and dull. Its inner radiance and willpower decline. Such a mind is no longer able to exercise its mastery over the body. As a result, the body's innate ability to heal itself is damaged. Vishoka Meditation reverses this process by restoring the body's internal ecology and the natural vibrancy and clarity of the mind.

From Despair to Self-Conquest

A tale told and retold in India for thousands of years gives us a glimpse of the scope of Vishoka Meditation and its transformative power. This is the story of Dhruva, a young man born and raised in an extremely dysfunctional family. Yet Dhruva went on to become a legendary ruler whose name is associated with inner stability, indomitable will, courage, clarity, enthusiasm, and lasting happiness.

••••••••••••

Dhruva's father was a king with two wives. Dhruva was the son of the first wife, who came from a kingdom of moderate power, wealth, and influence. She was humble, kind, and somewhat innocent. But the second wife, Dhruva's stepmother, was beautiful, proud, and ambitious. She came from a powerful royal family and exerted enormous influence on her husband and his courtiers.

Having subdued her husband, the second queen accumulated power and basked in the glamour that accompanies a sovereign. But Dhruva's presence haunted her. He was the first son of the king's first wife and, according to the law of the land, was the king's rightful heir. The second queen's hunger for power, prestige, and attention grew until she found the presence of Dhruva and his mother intolerable. By creating scandalous rumors and feeding them skillfully, she turned the king, his courtiers, and everyone else against the pair and soon succeeded in ousting them from the palace.

But the misery she inflicted on Dhruva and his mother did not end with depriving them of their home. She made sure that the life of the homeless pair was more painful than death. Fearing her wrath, the king's subjects denied mother and son shelter and food. Deprivation and humiliation became a way of life.

What could be worse for a mother than watching helplessly as her son is humiliated? What could be worse for a son than not being able to do anything when his mother is insulted before his eyes? How intensely painful it must have been for the young prince, who knew he was the rightful heir to the kingdom, to be treated worse than a stray dog by his own people. How can someone in such a situation be free from the torments of animosity and revenge? How can someone who has been betrayed by his own father ever trust anyone? How can a person drowning in a bottomless sea of dejection and sorrow retain any love for life? Caught in a whirlpool of misery and not knowing what else to do, the young man quietly abandoned his mother and vanished.

Meanwhile Narada, one of the most revered masters of his time, visited the kingdom. Narada had been Dhruva's grandfather's best friend. He heard about the nasty dynamics in the palace and the misery that weighed on the young prince so heavily that he had shut himself off from his only remaining source of hope, his own mother. Deeply moved, Narada set out to search for Dhruva. Eventually, he found him roaming aimlessly in a part of the forest where no human dared enter unprotected, a sure sign that the young man had lost his will to live.

Dhruva recognized Narada immediately, and this unexpected encounter opened a floodgate of childhood memories. He remembered his grandfather and a palace abounding in love, care, and nurturance, and he remembered what had transpired after his grandfather died. For his part, Narada saw this grief-stricken man from inside out. He saw how decrepit Dhruva had become—his youthful vibrancy had been almost completely consumed by his lack of trust in himself, trust in his kinsmen, trust in providence, and trust in truth and justice.

Narada was determined to help Dhruva shake off his sorrow and grief and reclaim the power he needed to become happy and self-trusting once more. The sage knew this was a delicate matter. The young man was weak and had become frail. He had nowhere to live and nothing to eat. His heart was shrunken and his mind scattered. But worst of all, he had lost hope.

Narada knew that this young man first needed assurance that someone loved him. He must realize he was not alone so he could regain a sense of belongingness. He must also reclaim his physical vitality and mental clarity. Narada knew that because the emotional injuries caused by his family and the rest of the world were so fresh, it was too early to talk about discovering the deeper causes of his afflictions. The first step was to help this young man restore his sense of normalcy. Only then would it be possible to inspire him to discover the tools and means to find and conquer all adversaries, including those that are hardest to defeat—fear, doubt, anger, enmity, and regret. The methodology Narada used to help Dhruva achieve this goal came to be known as Vishoka Meditation.

Narada led the young prince through a process that enabled him to replenish his body and restore the balance of his mind. He taught Dhruva how to protect his mind from the emotional storms arising from deep-rooted afflicting memories. He taught him breathing techniques for healing his mind, heart, and body, and for restoring his internal ecology.

This breath-driven quest brought Dhruva to a point where he could stop his mind from spinning and allow it to become still. From that place of stillness he was able to see the subtle cause of his fear, anger, sorrow, and grief. He saw clearly that his father and stepmother were simply the triggers, not the actual cause. With this awareness he could now easily erase the long list of complaints his mind had been nurturing. This gave him great comfort, for now he realized that he did not need to beg the world to grant him justice. He did not need his family, friends, or anyone else to assure him that he was safe from his adversaries. Free from fear, doubt, anger, enmity, grief, and hopelessness, he now understood he had the ability to create his own destiny.

The scriptures tell us that it took six months for Dhruva to move from utter despair to complete stillness. As soon as he stopped fighting his inner enemies, the process of reconciliation at home began. His father and stepmother recognized their folly.

They made every attempt to bring Dhruva back to the palace, but he stayed firm in his resolve to make himself stronger, clearer, and independently happy. The prospect of reclaiming the love, respect, power, and dignity he rightfully deserved was not as alluring as discovering how freedom from inner conflict resolves conflicts in the external world. He continued the practice and eventually reached the place in his own heart that abounds with supernal bliss. He recognized that the state of consciousness infused with this bliss is the pure being, the eternal self.

Dhruva realized this is the very axis of existence. The world of pleasure and pain, gain and loss, honor and insult, victory and defeat, and even birth and death, revolves around it, as does every event and every experience. He understood that constant awareness of this reality enables us to navigate all calamities joyfully. There is no greater achievement than finding and retaining our connection with this reality. It is only when we are disconnected from this pure being that our relationships with our friends and foes become confusing. All quests and conquests begin from here. All commotions and defeats begin in the absence of this connection.

Dhruva's story concludes with an extraordinary experience—he rose above his physical and mental level of awareness and was totally absorbed in the collective consciousness of the universe. The wall that separates an individual from the universal self collapsed. He was the world and the world was him. Past, present, and future became a continuum. Mundane and sacred were no longer separate. Dhruva saw creation as an extension of its creator. This experience was so thrilling that the subtle thread of his breath came to a complete halt.

Because this spontaneous breath retention occurred when

the world had become an integral part of Dhruva's conscious-ness, the breath of life in the entire world ceased. All living be-ings began to suffocate. The forces of nature and high-caliber souls and divinities petitioned the creator to bring Dhruva back to normal consciousness, so living beings could regain their breath. Thus Vishnu, the all-pervading creator and protector of all, pulled Dhruva from this profound meditative state and blessed him with the highest degree of power, prestige, honor, wisdom, stability, and endurance. During his life he ruled the earth. At death he was awarded immortality and shines in the night sky as Polaris, the North Star. Thus, in Indian astrology, the name for the pole star is Dhruva.

Meeting Diverse Needs: Three Stages of Practice

Like Dhruva's journey, Vishoka Meditation begins with the right understanding of pain and sorrow and ends with lasting joy and fulfillment. The sizeable gap between where it begins and where it ends is filled with a series of techniques and prac-tices designed to help us overcome our weaknesses and reclaim our innate strength.

We all have unique strengths and weaknesses. Our strug-gles and aspirations are also unique. These varying degrees of strength and weakness and the unique qualities of our struggles and aspirations play a crucial role in defining the goals and objec-tives of our practice. Thus great masters like Buddha and Patan-jali have delineated the entire practice of Vishoka Meditation in three different stages. The following story, drawn from the *Lotus*

Sutra (*Sad-Dharma Pundarika Sutra*), demonstrates how different stages of this practice apply to different groups of people and how the initial stages serve as a foundation for those that follow.

•••••••••••

One day, with the intention of immersing himself in a deep state of meditation, Buddha fixed his seat on a hilltop known as Griddha Kuta. Before entering the ultracognitive state of meditation he glanced at the world inhabited by humans. It was mingled with joy and sorrow. Everyone was busy—some willingly, some unwillingly, some joyfully, and others painfully. Everyone carried a noisy mind. Complaints and regrets accompanied almost everyone, and their love for life was contaminated by fear of death.

Buddha closed his eyes and entered a realm of stillness from where he could hear everything—even the slightest rustle of an anxious mind. He found every heart begging for relief from sorrow and grief. He became established in his pure essence and resolved to help these suffering souls. Instantly, a dazzling light emerged from the center of his forehead, filling the three realms: earth, heaven, and the sky in between. Startled by this light, one of the future buddhas, Maitreya, approached the ancient buddha Manjushri and said, "I am certain this is the light of Shakyamuni Buddha. O Enlightened One, you have witnessed such extraordinary phenomena before and know what it portends. With the dispersion of this light today, what does Buddha intend to accomplish?"

Manjushri replied, "This is the light of the wisdom contained in the *Lotus Sutra*. It is imbued with limitless compassion and propelled by the intention of eradicating pain and sorrow. This light is known by several names. It does not tolerate darkness and so is called *jyotishmati*, self-luminous light. It empowers people to transcend (*vi*) all forms of fear, sorrow, and grief (*shoka*), and so is called *vishoka*. It enables seekers to cross the river of mind and reach the other shore of pure consciousness, and so is called *taraka*. It showers the nectar of spiritually up-lifting thoughts, and so is called *dharma megha*, the cloud of virtues. This is the mother of true fortune. There is no end to the glory of this light. It is the light of hope. This light marks a historic event in the universe. Let us join Shakyamuni Buddha in person and witness the skill with which he delivers this wisdom."

With this, Manjushri, Maitreya, and a host of other bud-dhas and bodhisattvas descended from their heavenly abodes and joined the audience awaiting the sermon of Buddha on the peak of Griddha Kuta.

Buddha opened his eyes like one who is drunk. His mind still lingered within. Despite his intention to bring liberation to suffering souls with his enlightening words, his tongue did not move. Sensing that Buddha's perfectly still, inwardly flowing mind needed some support to turn outward, his senior student, Sariputra, skillfully drew Buddha's attention with a question: "Lord, where have you been and what made you return to this world, which serves no purpose for you?"

Words as sweet as honey rolled from Buddha's lips: "I was in the world of vishoka, a space of consciousness where fear, anger, doubt, regret, worry, and sorrow do not exist. Absolute peace was my companion. The joy of meditation was my food. The pulsation of pure being was my breath. This all-consuming blissful state was fueling my desire to enter *maha nirvana*. Then a thought flashed: Many buddhas have come before me. All had a choice about whether or not to be part of this mortal world, and each of them chose to be part of it.

"What caused them to embrace the same world they had renounced after such a great struggle? Like me, all of them had attained *prajna-paramita*, perfection in intuitive wisdom. Their power of memory had expanded to infinity. They were able to remember every experience related to their own life and everyone else's with perfection and precision. The knowledge of past, present, and future stood before them intact. They remembered their struggles when they lived in the world. They remembered how painful it was, but also how that same world provided the tools and means to transcend their pain. These buddhas were fully aware of the many buddhas and bodhisattvas who had contributed to their buddhahood. Gratitude to previous buddhas and compassion for those suffering from the afflictions rampant in the world compelled these great souls to return and share the knowledge that liberated them. I must do the same. Thus I returned to the world."

"Enlighten us with your liberating knowledge, O Master."

Buddha remained quiet. Sariputra urged him again. This time the expression on Buddha's face clearly conveyed his unwillingness to respond to Sariputra's question.

With humility and firmness Sariputra spoke: "You have proclaimed me to be your eldest son; thus you have given me the responsibility to serve your children. For my sake and for the sake of those whom I am supposed to serve, please enlighten us with your liberating knowledge."

Buddha spoke: "Our core being is pure and pristine. Absolute stillness is intrinsic to it. It is the ultimate source of peace and happiness. It is the source of true protection and nourishment. Living in the light of this knowledge is enlightenment. The life of an enlightened being is free of fear and regret. An enlightened person lives simply and effortlessly. Groping our way through the world without this knowledge is bondage. The life of an ignorant person is full of fear and regret. His is a life of turmoil and stress."

While Buddha was speaking, a famous bodhisattva known as Prajnakuta joined the audience. When Buddha asked what had brought him there, the bodhisattva replied, "With your blessings and the blessings of my master, I am free from disease, old age, and death. Now without any impediment I have decided to enter the most blessed state of buddhahood. Please guide me. How may I reach that state of consciousness?"

Buddha responded, "I am glad you came to me at a time when the sky above and around us is filled with celestial beings, siddhas, devas, buddhas, and bodhisattvas. Let me invoke Manjushri. He will guide you on your path to buddhahood."

Manjushri materialized instantly and exchanged greetings with Buddha. When Manjushri was seated, the bodhisattva asked, "How many people have you guided into the realm of buddhahood?"

Instantly thousands of shining beings, each sitting on a thousand-petaled lotus, descended from the sky. Pointing at them, Manjushri said, "All these and numberless thousands more."

The bodhisattva asked, "What is that wisdom that led them to this exalted state?"

"It is the wisdom of the lotus of the heart, the essence of the *Lotus Sutra*," Manjushri replied.

The bodhisattva said, "This sutra is extremely profound, subtle, and hard to comprehend. I am yet to be convinced that anyone can grasp the essence of this wisdom."

Manjushri responded, "At the age of eight, the daughter of

Nagaraja received and fully absorbed the essence of this wisdom. She was born with a pure and pristine mind. In the blink of an eye she comprehends thousands of questions and their answers. All virtues abide with her."

The bodhisattva argued, "How is this possible? Even Shakyamuni Buddha had to work hard. How can anyone—especially a woman—attain perfection in buddhahood with less effort than Buddha himself?"

At this the daughter of Nagaraja appeared. She bowed her head to Buddha and sat next to him.

Bewildered, the bodhisattva continued, "There are five things women cannot achieve. Among them is the unmoving and undecaying state of bodhisattva. Of this I am certain."

Hearing this, Nagaraja's daughter extended her hand to Buddha. A shining gem rested on her palm. Buddha accepted it instantly. She looked at the bodhisattva and said, "See how happily the Lord accepted my gift. This solves your problem."

She transformed herself into a man, then became genderless and disappeared.

Buddha told the bodhisattva, "You have convinced yourself that attaining buddhahood is not an easy task. That is what is making it hard for you to achieve it. Furthermore, your belief that women cannot achieve it is a reflection of your strong identity as a man. Only after you transcend all identities, including gender identity, are you entitled to achieve the state of buddhahood."

Buddha then gave his final instructions: "The gem Nagaraja's daughter offered me is an embodiment of all virtues. Attachment to meritorious deeds and their fruits is the subtlest of all afflictions. You nullify the effects of your painful actions by performing good deeds. Yet only when you renounce your identification as a spiritually evolved person can you enter the world of buddhahood."

Humbled, the bodhisattva bowed his head to Buddha in gratitude and left for an extended meditation.

Buddha turned to Sariputra and the audience. "What I just taught to this bodhisattva and how I taught it is *buddhayana*, the path that leads directly to buddhahood. A person established in this state of consciousness is absolutely free from all pain and sorrow, as well as their cause. There is no room for rigidity on this path. No standard rules or techniques define it. A skillful teacher identifies the subtlest affliction blocking the individual aspirant's entry to buddhahood and skillfully helps remove that affliction. Thereafter, in almost no time, the aspirant becomes established in the essential nature of buddhahood.

"But not everyone is ready to tread this path. I called upon Manjushri; Manjushri called upon the daughter of Nagaraja. They emerged from thin air. That is an extraordinary event. In response to the sheer intention of Manjushri, a host of buddhas and bodhisattvas emerged. That is an extraordinary event. Nagaraja's daughter materialized the self-luminous gem and transformed herself into a man and then became genderless. That too is an extraordinary event.

"There was a purpose behind all these events. First, the obstacle preventing the bodhisattva from reaching buddhahood was so subtle it could not be removed by ordinary means. Second, I wanted the people in the audience to know that beyond this material plane there is a reality more potent and more real than our phenomenal world. Knowing this reality and becoming part of it is supremely rewarding.

"But not everyone understands this or has the willingness

to understand it. Most people have neither the time nor the motivation to know the reality beyond their familiar world. This world comprises family and friends, competitors and enemies. It is made of numberless relationships. The law of change, the force behind birth and death, and everything that falls in between rules this world.

"In this world, people experience disease, old age, poverty, oppression, exploitation, and physical and mental decrepitude. They also experience the pleasures associated with good health, youth, prosperity, and power. People from all walks of life are familiar with fear, anger, doubt, regret, grief, and a sense of worthlessness. Rich and poor, young and old, healthy and sick—all are busy avoiding pain and seeking happiness. And they are doing it within the confines of their familiar world. Transcending this world and becoming part of the world where pain and sorrow do not exist is beyond their comprehension. For such people, the knowledge Manjushri, Nagaraja's daughter, and I shared with the bodhisattva Prajnakuta serves no purpose.

"Human beings can be divided into three categories. People like Prajnakuta belong to the first category. They are highly evolved souls. Their problems and the solution to their problems are subtle. They are endowed with a high degree of comprehension and determination. When their problems are revealed, they are delighted. Without any help from external sources, they rise above their subtle afflictions and reach buddhahood.

"People in the second category are enlightened enough to know they have problems and to some extent also know the cause, but they lack clarity, inner strength, and courage. They need help from external sources—a teacher, a scripture, a spiritually uplifting environment, or divine providence. Their journey is marked by ups and downs, but every step in the journey adds to their clarity, inner strength, and courage. They conquer the adversaries detectable by the mind and intellect. Eventually they join the league of bodhisattvas, the first category of aspirants.

"The third category is made of people so immersed in their day-to-day existence that they have neither the time nor the energy to reflect on life's painful conditions, let alone discover the causes of those conditions. Many people in this category do not even know they are miserable and need help. They are prisoners of their circumstances. Some are prisoners of their inflated ego and others of an inferiority complex. Some are prisoners of material poverty and others of inner poverty. Some are prisoners of a diseased body and others of a confused mind.

"While living in these prisons, they cry, complain, and pray for help. Lofty teachings and techniques leading to buddhahood are meaningless to them. They need relief from their current pain and sorrow. They need assurance that they are not alone. They need love and nurturance, and they need to regain their self-trust. Their hope has to be rekindled. In short, someone has to pull them out of that grim and hopeless space and show them that freedom from pain and sorrow is possible. A person capable of doing that is a true teacher. And the technique he uses to accomplish it is the perfect technique.

"The world is primarily composed of people belonging to this third category. Even the most blessed ones—powerful, rich, and enlightened people—pass through this stage. The skill with which people manage the trials and tribulations of this stage determines when and how they will join the league of those in the other two categories. Everyone is born with the potential to conquer the long chain of pain and sorrow, and everyone has the potential to find and become established in lasting peace and happiness. Those who are free from physical pain will have the energy and willingness to find the cause and the cure for their mental distress. Those who are free from mental distress will have enough clarity and enthusiasm to discover the cause and cure for the subtle afflictions that throw them into the torrent of birth and death.

"My teachings always begin with those who are suffering and end with those aspiring to become Buddha. These teachings are grounded in direct experience. For a seeker of truth, knowledge without experience is a burden. Experiential knowledge alone has transformative power. Experience comes from practice. Practice bears fruit when it is methodical.

"The practice that enabled me to discover the cause and the cure for pain and sorrow and made me Buddha comprises a series of techniques. In the initial stage, these techniques help a person find immediate relief from pain and sorrow. In the intermediate stage, they induce mental clarity and focus. They enable the meditator to see the true nature of the reality characterized by mortality and the true nature of the reality that transcends mortality. At the advanced stage, they lift the final veil of illusion and infuse the mind and heart of the meditator with extraordinary willpower and determination. When this veil lifts, the meditator neither grieves over what is past nor worries about what is to come. That is perfect freedom—the ground for lasting peace and happiness.

"This series of techniques is practiced in three successive stages and is part of a complete and comprehensive system of meditation. This system of meditation has a definite goal. It is for discovering the mind and its binding and releasing forces. It is for giving the mind the power to rule over the body and the short-lived experiences of the phenomenal world. It is for living in the world and remaining above it. It is for living fully, with purpose and meaning."

Nurturing the Body and Empowering the Mind

The system of meditation Buddha described is the heart and soul of yoga. It derives its power from the experiences of masters like Narada and Buddha and thousands of others who came before and after them. These experiences reveal a universal truth: there is suffering in the world; there is a cause of suffering; suffering can end; and there is a way to reach that end. Suffering is an integral part of life for those who do not know the source of life or what sustains it. Suffering is insurmountable for those who do not know what propels us toward sickness, old age, and death.

The experiences of the masters also reveal that the cause and the cure for human suffering are buried deep in our mind. A clear, calm, one-pointed, inwardly flowing mind has the capacity to discover both cause and cure. A confused, restless, scattered, and outwardly running mind has no capacity to discover either the cause of pain and sorrow or the cure. That is why every master in the past prescribed a system of meditation designed to cultivate a clear, calm, one-pointed, and inwardly flowing mind.

In different times and places experienced masters have used this system of meditation to help their students overcome their most pressing concerns. Some students used this technique to overcome grief and others to overcome anger. Some applied it to calm their nervous system and replenish their depleted body. Some used it to focus their mind and sharpen their intellect.

Some found it an effective tool for cultivating love for themselves and for life, and for overcoming the pain of abandonment. Some used it to uncover the greatest of all mysteries—the mind—and to gain access to the mind's limitless powers. Some used it for healing and others for enlightenment.

The practice is always introduced in response to our personal needs as well as the overarching needs of our society. There will always be some fortunate souls aspiring to become Buddha and light the flame of love, wisdom, and compassion. But the majority of us are not yet there. We are embroiled in a fight with an army of formidable enemies: fear, anger, hatred, grief, and feelings of unworthiness. We are questioning life's purpose. At the physical level we are dealing with a body working hard to rid itself of a broad range of toxins. To manage pain we turn to drugs, but soon find them consuming us instead. Some of us suffer from physical and mental conditions that have their source in traumatic experiences. In short, we are in dire need of adopting a plan that nurtures our body and re-empowers our mind. That plan is Vishoka Meditation.

The practice of Vishoka Meditation has three distinct stages. The first stage is composed of a series of techniques for awakening the healing power of the breath and the self-guiding power of the mind. With the help of these techniques, we refine the breath, which first requires learning to breathe deeply, smoothly, and silently. When the pause between the inhalation and the exhalation is removed, the breath becomes smooth and even. This smooth and even breathing leads to the harmonious functioning of our brain, nervous system, endocrine system, and internal organs. The body becomes a perfect vessel for containing a healthy and harmonious mind. A refined breath frees the mind from distractions and disturbances arising from bodily systems and sense organs. A mind free from physical disturbances captures the opportunity to awaken its inner intelligence.

The goal of the first stage of Vishoka Meditation is to unite the mind and the breath for a minimum of 10 minutes. This 10-minute uninterrupted union is crucial. In these 10 minutes, the mind and the breath rediscover their innate relationship: the mind discovers the breath is its protector and provider; the breath discovers the mind is its guide and the executor of its plans. Together they understand their role in healing, nurturing, and protecting the body. They also understand how they can employ the body and sense organs to find the fulfillment the soul is seeking. This uninterrupted 10-minute union empowers the mind and the breath to discover the deeper causes of inner unrest. It also empowers the mind to see its own self-defeating tendencies, and fills it with confidence that it can conquer those tendencies.

This first stage enables us to recognize that all miseries are self-created and that we have the power to transcend them. It fills us with confidence that inner peace and happiness is our birthright and we have the capacity to claim it. In short, this initial stage introduces us to ourselves. Thereafter, the genuine desire arises to discover and experience our own grandeur and its relationship with a higher reality. Our desire to know and achieve life's higher purpose becomes stronger than our worries about day-to-day affairs. Our desire to experience the richness of life drives away the fear of losing what we have, including our most precious possession—life itself. This newly born desire also drives away our uncertainty about achieving objects we do not have. In other words, our petty desires, concerns, and worries are replaced with meaningful, well-focused desires. Such desires are charged with the energy of illumination and motivation.

In the light of these desires we are inspired to know what lies beyond our day-to-day world. We want to know what brings us here and what guides us during the crucial moments of birth and death. Who accompanies us from breath to breath? Who fills us with confidence that we will reach our destination? In whose absence do we feel lost? In short, we become deeply interested in knowing our essential self and its relationship with its creator. We want to know how to reach the state of permanent safety, clarity, and self-realization, from where there is no possibility of falling back into a world of doubt, fear, uncertainty, and confusion. This marks the culmination of the first stage of Vishoka Meditation and the beginning of the second stage.

The second stage is composed of techniques that enable the mind to experience its intrinsic joy (*vishoka*) and luminosity (*jyotishmati*). Mantra is the hallmark of this stage. The mantra assists the mind in destroying the veil that hides its intrinsic luminosity. In the glow of its own inner light, the mind is able to see the subtle causes of its afflicting thoughts and tendencies. The power of mantra enables the mind to face and conquer those deep-rooted tendencies. Furthermore, mantra empowers the mind to identify and embrace its positive and noble tendencies. Most importantly, the power of mantra guides the mind to enter the cave of the heart and discover its eternal friend, the Divine Being. Practically speaking, this stage is mantra meditation. Because it results in the blossoming of our core being, masters like Buddha and Patanjali call it meditation on the lotus of the heart.

This second stage takes us to a place where we realize that the Divine Being always accompanies us. It has been with us before we were born, it is with us now, and it will continue to be with us even after death. We are never alone. The giver of life is our protector and provider. The experience brought by this stage of meditation destroys the ground for questioning the eternity of the life force we embody.

In the face of this experience, our doubt and fear vanish forever. The phenomenal world characterized by victory and defeat, gain and loss, honor and insult, and union and separation loses its grip on our mind. While living in the world, we still endeavor to thrive but without losing sight of the everlasting reality. The scriptures call this state *jivanmukti*, freedom here and now. This stage gives us a highly refined, empowered mind, which enables us to intuit the presence of the reality that lies beyond the senses and discursive mind. This engenders a craving to immerse ourselves in that reality, and marks the culmination of the second stage and the beginning of the final stage.

The third stage is technically known as Sri Vidya. Sri Vidya is the ultimate distillation of tantric and Vedic knowledge and experience. The practice of Sri Vidya is richer and more complex than the first two stages of Vishoka Meditation. It comprises tantric methods of awakening kundalini, piercing the chakras, meditating on highly potent mantras, and applying alchemy. This stage enables us to see the mind as an extension of the divine in us, and the body as an extension of our mind. Similarly, we see this universe as a manifestation of the primordial Divine Being.

The realization that we are born as a human, that we have a wonderful mind and body, and that we are living in a world saturated with divine essence fills us with elation. Reaching this state of elation and maintaining it is the heart and soul of the third stage. We reach this stage primarily through grace rather than self-effort. However, we are able to receive and retain grace only when we have done our best to practice the first two stages. This volume is a comprehensive guide to the series of practices that constitute the crucial first stage of Vishoka Meditation.

CHAPTER 2
The Practice of
Vishoka Meditation

Success in meditation rests on our ability to unite the mind with the breath. When united with a healthy breath, the mind becomes healthy, but it becomes unhealthy when united with an unhealthy breath. For a fruitful meditation we need a healthy mind, which is why yogis regard breath as the heart and soul of meditation.

Healthy breathing is marked by a smooth, serene flow. There is no labor involved—inhalation and exhalation follow each other seamlessly. This makes the mind relaxed, fresh, and vibrant. It is naturally inclined to be focused and creative. Unhealthy breathing, on the other hand, is noisy, shallow, shaky, and erratic. There is an unconscious pause between inhalation and exhalation. Unhealthy breathing makes the mind dull, lazy, and anxious. It becomes agitated at the slightest provocation. This kind of mind is easily scattered and quickly becomes pessimistic, confused, and fearful.

Vishoka Meditation begins with establishing healthy breathing and cultivating a peaceful, one-pointed, inwardly flowing mind. This inwardly flowing mind is then brought to a focal point at the center of the forehead, one of the most sensitive regions in the body. Because the center of the forehead is the first point of focus in Vishoka Meditation, this center and the part of the brain corresponding to it are the first to be nourished by the practice, which is propelled by the nourishing power of the breath.

As the practice gains momentum, the bond between the breath and the mind becomes stronger, and our power of concentration increases. We become acutely aware of our internal states. We are able to see the cause of our physical and mental disturbances as well as the cure. A strong bond between mind and breath sharpens our mental faculties, and we become cognizant of our pure being. In the light of pure being, our numberless personae melt away. The burden of our preconceived notions and preoccupations is lifted. The joy of pure being frees the mind from painful memories of the past and anxiety about the future. This empowers us to live in the present, free from fear and uncertainty. Once we have achieved this freedom, we can go on to discover the limitless gifts buried in our own body and mind and in the larger world of which we are an integral part.

Uniting Breath and Mind

In the normal course of life the mind is constantly attending one train of thought or another. All thoughts—positive or negative, purposeful or aimless—drain the mind's vitality and mar its stillness and tranquility. The mind becomes tired and depleted, which leads to irritability. An irritable mind is prone to angry and irrational thoughts, depleting it further. To stop this process and replenish the mind, we must withdraw it from the endless chain of thoughts and unite it with the breath. This is accomplished with the help of a unique breathing practice known as *aharana pranayama*—a necessary step in laying the foundation for Vishoka Meditation.

Aharana means "to bring back." Aharana pranayama is a breathing technique designed to bring the mind back to the body, its home base. This can be tricky and difficult. The mind is subtle and so are its interactions with the objects of its thoughts. The instant we think of withdrawing our mind from a particular place, time, or concern, the mind goes there. Thus withdrawing the mind from one place, time, or concern at a time is a never-ending process. In the practice of aharana pranayama, therefore, the emphasis is not on gathering the scattered pieces of the mind but on becoming aware of the place where the mind is supposed to be—at home in the body.

Every nook and cranny of the body is filled with the power of the mind. But when the mind is disturbed and dissipated, we do not feel its presence in our body in any significant way. Trying to become aware of our body with the help of a disturbed and dissipated mind is futile. However, there is a natural bond between the life force (*prana*) and the mind. Further, there is a greater concentration of the life force in certain regions of the body—such as the crown, the center of the forehead, the heart center, and the navel center. The instant we think of one of these centers, the mind rushes there. The primordial relationship between the life force and the mind gives the mind the impetus to collect its scattered forces and come into full view in these pranically charged centers. The natural bond between the mind and the life force allows the mind to stay at these centers with relatively little effort. The longer the mind stays there, the more nourished, peaceful, one-pointed, sharp, and aware it becomes. Furthermore, this newly found stability and patience give the mind a chance to taste the joy of being in the body.

The joy of resting in the body discourages the mind from running after worldly objects and concerns. At the same time, the long-cherished habit of embracing those objects and concerns encourages the mind to abandon the idea of resting in the body and prompts it to re-engage with worldly concerns. Aharana pranayama gives us a strategy for coping with this dilemma.

The practice of aharana pranayama begins at the center of the forehead. Practically speaking, becoming aware of the center of the forehead means feeling the combined flow of the breath and the mind there. We can maintain this awareness only as long as our habitual tendencies do not force the mind to wander away. The stronger our habitual tendencies, the more disturbed, stupefied, and distracted our mind. Such a mind will fail to stay at the center of the forehead for any significant period.

To manage this situation, we stay at the forehead center only for the time required to take three deep breaths. We breathe gently and smoothly. There is no noise or jerkiness in the breath. Although air travels inward toward the lungs when we inhale and outward when we exhale, during this practice our mind is oblivious of this anatomical dimension of breathing. Instead it is aware of the subtle pulsation of the non-physical dimension of breathing at the center of the forehead and is fully engaged in sensing that pulsation. This engagement allows the mind to unite itself with prana, the life force. After experiencing this union for three complete breaths, we deliberately move on to another pranic center.

From the standpoint of concentrating the life force, some pranic centers are more significant than others. When practicing aharana pranayama as part of Vishoka Meditation, we select only a few of these. The sequence in which the mind is allowed to travel and concentrate on these centers is significant. Bringing them into conscious awareness in the prescribed sequence enables the mind to become familiar with the general map of the pranic counterpart of the physical body. This sequence requires the mind to travel from the head to the perineum, and back, resting briefly at each pranic center, thus transforming the apparently abstract relationship between the body and the mind into a concrete experience. This process ensures that the mind is grounded in the body. The mind and the body are in full embrace—a necessary condition if we are to experience ourselves fully.

Aharana Pranayama

Begin aharana pranayama by bringing your awareness to the center of the forehead. While maintaining that awareness, take three smooth, deep breaths through your nose. (One inhalation and exhalation together constitute one breath.) Without putting any strain on your eyes or eyebrows, maintain awareness in the center of the forehead. This is an effortless process. When you are not aware of anything other than your sheer presence, by default you are aware of yourself in the center of your forehead. This awareness has no shape, size, or color. It is a formless feeling of self-existence.

Inhale and exhale into this formless field of self-awareness.

Absorption in this field is so deep you have no awareness of any other places or concerns. In fact, the state of mental absorption in the center of your forehead is so profound that you are barely aware of the rest of your body. This makes you oblivious of the physical dimension of breathing. With each breath, you are simply aware of waves of pranic energy arising from the center of the forehead and subsiding back into it.

After taking three smooth, deep breaths at the center of the forehead, bring your attention down to the eyebrow center and take one complete breath. Make sure you are fully relaxed and are not putting any strain on your eyes. Effortlessness—which translates into a relaxed state of awareness—applies to every focal point where you take your mind as part of aharana pranayama.

Next bring your attention to your eyes and take one complete breath. Then move on to your nostrils, throat, shoulders, upper arms, elbows, wrists, and palms, taking one complete breath at each place. Then bring your attention to your fingertips and take two deep breaths with your attention resting there. Next, move back to your palms, wrists, elbows, upper arms, and shoulders, taking one breath at each point. Then bring your attention to your throat, heart, bottom of the sternum, navel center, and pelvis—again taking one breath at each. Next, bring your attention to the perineum and take two breaths before moving back to the pelvis, navel center, bottom of the sternum, heart, throat, nostrils, eyes, center between the eyebrows, and center of the forehead, taking one breath at each. From the center of the forehead move to the crown center. Take three smooth, deep breaths at the crown center. This completes aharana pranayama.

Cultivating Inner Balance

There is another pranayama that is a necessary prelude to Vishoka Meditation. Known as *samikarana* (equalization), this breathing practice is designed to bring the body to a state of balance.

The ecology of the body is dependent on three factors: secretion, absorption, and rhythm. Too much, too little, or a disproportionate secretion of hormones, enzymes, and digestive juices disrupts the normal functions of our organs and systems, throwing the autonomic nervous system out of balance. This places enormous stress on the visceral organs—in particular, the liver, kidneys, heart, lungs, and reproductive and digestive organs—because they are forced to work harder to maintain the body's equilibrium. Poor absorption and metabolization of secretions also disrupt the body's equilibrium.

Rhythm is the third factor that plays a key role in the body's ecology. Following the law of nature, our breathing pattern changes every 90 minutes or so. For example, at any given time our breath flows more actively from one nostril and more passively from the other. This pattern switches approximately every 60–90 minutes: the active nostril becomes passive, and vice versa. Both nostrils flow equally only briefly during this transition. Similarly, when we sleep we dream for a period of time, then go into a state of deep sleep before returning to the dreaming state. During these transitions, there is a short period of extraordinary stillness, which far exceeds the tranquility of even deep sleep. This is how nature has designed rhythmic cycles of activity and rest for the body, breath, and mind.

A disruption in these natural cycles is the breeding ground

for physical and mental diseases. Our consciousness senses the potential for disease long before it manifests and becomes recognizable. At a level beyond our conscious awareness, our innate intelligence demands that our body and mind design and execute a strategy to circumvent this threat. Thus, while maintaining their normal functions, our body and mind work to prevent future problems. If sufficient physical, mental, and intuitive reserves are lacking, we fall prey to anxiety, which disrupts the healthy patterns of inhalation and exhalation. This leads to disturbance in our breathing at the level of cellular respiration, which in turn leads to subtle but potent psychoenergetic fluttering. According to the *Yoga Sutra*, this phenomenon engenders mental negativity (*daurmanasya*). In time, this mental negativity manifests as pain, and pain contaminates our enthusiasm for living fully.

Samikarana pranayama offers a solution to this long chain of problems. Because it is always preceded by aharana pranayama, the scattered forces of the mind have already been brought back to their home base, the body. A significant level of bonding has already been established between the mind and the breath. The mind and the breath have made a cursory survey of the body before samikarana pranayama begins.

In the tantric school of Sri Vidya, samikarana pranayama is a complete practice in its own right and is quite elaborate. However, as a prelude to Vishoka Meditation, the masters of the tradition have adopted only the first step of that more comprehensive practice. In this context, they prescribe 10 points of focus: the crown of the head, center of the forehead, center between the eyebrows, nostrils, throat, heart, bottom of the sternum, navel, pelvis, and perineum.

Unlike aharana pranayama, where we are instructed to take a

complete breath at different centers, here we breathe between the perineum and the fontanel without stopping at any point. In this regard, the entire practice can be divided into two parts: descending breath (*avaroha*) and ascending breath (*aroha*). We descend with an exhalation and ascend with an inhalation. Exhalation begins at the crown and terminates at the perineum; inhalation begins at the perineum and terminates at the crown. Exhalation and inhalation follow each other seamlessly—there is no pause at either termination point. The eight points between the perineum and the crown lie in the pathway of the descending and ascending breaths. We simply witness their presence without pausing. In other words, we consciously acknowledge the presence of these centers as the united current of mind and breath passes through them.

Samikarana Pranayama

Because aharana pranayama concludes with three breaths at the crown center, samikarana pranayama begins there. To mark the beginning of samikarana pranayama, take a smooth, deep breath, filling the region of the crown. As you exhale, feel the flow of breath descending from the crown center to the center of the forehead, eyebrow center, nostrils, throat center, heart center, bottom of the sternum, navel center, pelvis, and perineum. Without pausing at the perineum, begin inhaling and feel the flow of breath ascending from the perineum all the way to the crown center. While ascending, witness the presence of the breath in the regions of the pelvis, navel, bottom of the sternum, heart, throat, nostrils, eyebrow center, and center of the forehead, finally reaching the crown. Repeat the entire process 10 times.

Upon reaching the crown the 10th time, again begin to exhale but this time, instead of exhaling all the way to the perineum, observe the united flow of mind and breath descending from the crown through the forehead and the eyebrow center to the nostrils. Continue exhaling smoothly through the nostrils into a space stretching 6–9 inches in front of you. This is where, technically speaking, samikarana pranayama ends and the main body of Vishoka Meditation begins.

The seamless transition from samikarana pranayama to Vishoka Meditation is dependent on the quality of samikarana pranayama. The quality of samikarana pranayama, in turn, is directly proportional to how gently, smoothly, and deeply we breathe. The quality of gentle, smooth, and deep breathing is dependent on the unhindered, seamless flow of the inhalation and the exhalation. The longer and more involuntary the pause between the inhalation and the exhalation, the more effort is required to breathe after the pause. This effort degrades the quality of the breath.

In the normal course of breathing, there is always an unconscious pause between the exhalation and the inhalation. The pause between inhalation and exhalation is almost imperceptible, but there is a greater tendency to pause between the exhalation and the inhalation. In other words, it is easier to begin exhaling almost immediately after inhaling—the pause is so slight that the exhalation appears to follow the inhalation seamlessly. But it is more difficult to begin inhaling immediately after exhaling—there is a longer pause, and a noticeable degree of effort is involved in inhaling.

In the case of those with an unhealthy lifestyle, the pause between the exhalation and the inhalation is longer and deeper. They are prone to holding their breath out unconsciously for longer periods, and they do it more frequently. It is difficult for them to breathe effortlessly. Effort creates tension and tension leads to stress. Stressful breathing disrupts the peaceful function of the heart and brain, setting off a chain reaction that disrupts all the systems in the body, directly or indirectly. The solution lies in reducing the pause and allowing the inhalation and the exhalation to flow seamlessly. This objective is accomplished with the help of an ancillary practice known as *shvasa-prashvasa pravahi pranayama*, which will be described in detail in the next chapter.

The Context for Vishoka Meditation

Aharana and samikarana pranayamas are integral to Vishoka Meditation. From a practical standpoint, aharana pranayama merges into samikarana and samikarana merges into the main body of Vishoka. Samikarana pranayama ends with witnessing the combined forces of mind and breath flowing into the space in front of us with our last exhalation. Paying attention to this space and the exhalation moving into it is crucial to success in Vishoka Meditation. Let's consider why this is so important.

In the same way the earth is surrounded by its own atmosphere, each of us is surrounded by our own atmosphere. This is our personal space. It fills every nook and cranny of our body and extends 10 inches beyond it in every direction. Most of us are unaware that our inhalation originates in the space approximately 9 inches in front of our face, and that our exhalation is absorbed in the space approximately 9 inches in front of the nostrils. According to yogis, this lack of awareness causes us to lose ownership of the space where our breath begins and ends. Consequently, the innate capacity of this space to filter undesirable and unhealthy subtle vibrations declines. We become susceptible to the energies constantly emitted by the world outside our personal space.

As we progress in the practice of Vishoka Meditation, we become increasingly aware of our personal space. However, in the beginning we need to cultivate this awareness by familiarizing ourselves with a few of the uniquely circumscribed spots integral to this space: the opening of the nostrils, the inner corners of the eyes, the eyebrow center, and the center of the forehead. Only after we have cultivated sensitivity to these relatively concentrated spots in our personal space will we be able to bring the entire space into the fold of our conscious awareness.

Cultivating sensitivity to these concentrated spots is accomplished by aharana pranayama. Bringing the whole space into conscious awareness is accomplished by samikarana pranayama. The final part is accomplished at the end of samikarana pranayama, while we are exhaling into the personal space in front of us. Paying attention to the breath as it extends into this space and reaches the point from where the movement of inhalation can no longer be traced is one of the most important aspects of the practice of Vishoka Meditation. For the sake of convenience, let us call this point in space the zero point. Vishoka Meditation begins with an inhalation at the zero point.

The first uniquely circumscribed space we pull into our conscious awareness is the opening of the nostrils. This space is identified with the spot where we first feel the touch of incoming breath. Cultivating awareness of the first instant when the incoming breath touches this spot enables us to touch and feel both time and space. It enables us to register the time the breath touches the opening of the nostrils. It also enables us to register the exact spot where the breath touches the nostrils. Thus cognition of the time and space associated with breath is no longer an abstract theory but becomes a concrete experience. The concept of here and now becomes a living reality. This living reality becomes the ground for Vishoka Meditation.

In our tradition, the process of becoming aware of this uniquely charged space is called *sushumna* application. Sushumna application activates the central pranic current known as *sushumna nadi*. It forces our vast range of bioenergies to coalesce around this central nadi. Once this central pranic current is activated, the mind has little or no motivation to attend distracting thoughts.

There are three more centers to be pulled into conscious awareness: the center corresponding to the inner corners of the eyes (the medial canthi), the center between the eyebrows, and the center of the forehead. Our success in becoming aware of these centers is always in direct proportion to our success in sushumna application.

These three centers are close to each other anatomically. The space corresponding to them houses an intricate network of nerves, which communicates with every part of the brain. These centers have a significant influence on the balanced functions of the brain and the brain's command over the body, but that is not the main reason we pull them into conscious awareness. From the practitioner's standpoint, these centers are highly concentrated reservoirs of prana.

The relationship between prana and mind is timeless and eternal. In a disturbed, distracted, stupefied, and confused state, the mind is not aware of its eternal and nurturing friend. Pulling these centers into our conscious awareness and letting the mind pass through them provides the mind with an opportunity to know it is not alone—it is accompanied by the life force. This awareness becomes vivid when the mind passes through these highly concentrated pranic fields. Furthermore, when we breathe through these centers as a part of meditation, the mind gathers pranic elixir to heal and rejuvenate itself emotionally, karmically, and spiritually. As the process of collecting and imbibing the elixir is repeated with each breath, the mind becomes clearer, calmer, sharper, and more joyful. That is the kind of mind we need to defeat our afflicting thoughts.

The first of these three centers, the inner corners of the eyes, serves as a gateway to the second center. And the second—the eyebrow center—is the doorway to the third, the center of the forehead. The subtle quality of each of these centers is slightly different.

The quality of the pranic force at the inner corners of the eyes is predominantly joyful. In yogic language, prana here is saturated with "honey." The experience of joy unique to this center is deeply nourishing. It subdues the roaming tendencies of the mind arising from deep-rooted afflictions. The mind loses its taste for painful thoughts and effortlessly lets go of unpleasant and undesirable thoughts and feelings.

The quality of the pranic force at the eyebrow center is distinguished by its natural capacity to capture the mind and pull it gently inward. Energetically, this center is stronger than the center corresponding to the inner corners of the eyes. The joyful feeling filling the space at the inner corners of the eyes tempts the mind to linger there. But because the mind is united with the breath, in due course the mind reaches the eyebrow center. Although part of the mind is still engaged in imbibing the elixir at the inner corners of the eyes, the inward flow at the eyebrow center now becomes more pronounced. This inward pull impels the mind to quickly absorb as much nurturing elixir as possible and join the united currents of mind and breath at the eyebrow center.

The eyebrow center is the place where two prominent pranic currents—*ida* and *pingala*—merge. In the yoga tradition these currents are the energetic counterparts of the sympathetic and parasympathetic nervous systems. When these two opposing forces are brought to a state of balance, the mind is neither hyperactive nor slothful, but infused with profound quietude. This quietude is mingled with the joy gathered at the inner corners of the eyes. This joyfully active, quiet mind, combined with the breath, is described as sushumna. This extremely subtle pranic current is the most potent means of opening the door to the deepest level of experience. The mind drops all its defenses and joyfully accepts the idea of traveling inward.

Once the mind reaches the eyebrow center, the urgency for resolving issues pertaining to the mundane world fades. The innate intelligence of the eyebrow center reorganizes our priorities. Now we know instinctively that our top priority is reaching our true home and resting there. The same instinct guides our mind to our true home—the center of the forehead.

"The center of the forehead" refers to the space housing our brain and is not to be confused with a concrete physical location. It encompasses the space filling every nook and cranny of the brain, as well as the space extending approximately nine inches around the head. The focal point of this center is the space housing the cerebral cortex, most importantly, the frontal lobe. In yogic literature it is known as the *ajna chakra*, the command center.

The ajna chakra is a highly concentrated pranic field that constantly supplies the nourishment our consciousness needs to employ and monitor our physical and psychospiritual faculties.

The parts of the brain located in the domain of the ajna chakra receive and process sensory information. This is where conscious decisions regarding the objective world are made. In other words, we perceive the objective world through the lens of the ajna chakra and respond as it dictates. This chakra and its physical counterparts are continuously interfacing with two worlds—the world outside and the world inside. They contact the objects of the external world through the senses and the objects of the inner world through our retentive power.

As long as the vitality, strength, stamina, and agility of this center are intact, we are able to maintain our mastery over both the objective world and the inner world made of numberless memories. But when this center and the corresponding parts of the brain become weak, we are at the mercy of external and internal turmoil. Our capacity to employ and discipline our senses plummets. Our cortical brain continues to be bombarded with sensory input, but we have little or no capacity to selectively retrieve and process our memories and use them to make wise decisions. Thus the debility of this center and the parts of the brain corresponding to it become the breeding ground for a disturbed, stupefied, distracted, anxious, and confused mind. Healing and rejuvenating the ajna chakra is crucial to both our worldly endeavors and our spiritual aspirations. We accomplish this by allowing the combined forces of breath and mind to travel from the eyebrow center to the ajna chakra, and holding them there until their union matures.

Centuries of observation have led the yogis to conclude

that the minimum time necessary for the union of the mind and the pranic force to mature is the time required to take 12 breaths. The duration of one inhalation and exhalation during deep, dreamless sleep is considered to be the average length of our breath. Yogis use the length of the breath during deep sleep as a standard measurement because our breathing pattern changes from moment to moment when we are awake. For example, when we are excited or frightened, our breath quickens, and when we are relaxed, we breathe slowly, but when we are in deep, dreamless sleep, our breathing pattern settles and does not fluctuate significantly. During deep sleep, a healthy adult takes 15–20 breaths per minute (approximately 4 seconds per breath). Thus the mind and the pranic force must stay together for a minimum of 48 seconds (the time required to take 12 breaths) to absorb the effect of their union.

As we have seen, the pranic force and its innate intelligence have different transformative powers at the inner corners of the eyes, the eyebrow center, and the center of the forehead. For example, if the mind can disconnect from its roaming tendencies and remain focused on the space at and between the inner corners of the eyes for at least 48 seconds, the experience of sweetness unique to this center will be strong enough to defeat sensory charms, which make the mind restless.

When our concentration increases with practice and we are able to remain aware of the united flow of mind and breath at any one of these pranic centers for 12 times longer than 48 seconds (approximately 9.6 minutes), we gain mastery even over a mind heavily influenced by deep-rooted habits, addictions, and unconscious afflicting behaviors. When we are able to hold our mind on a pranic center for approximately 9.6 minutes, an amazing shift in consciousness occurs. As soon as we reach this stage, the effort-driven meditator in us moves effortlessly in the direction of mastery. Until we hit this 9.6-minute mark, all the struggles, trials, temptations, and tribulations continually appear, disappear, and reappear.

Mastering the Ajna Chakra

With this in mind, let us revisit the importance of cultivating a robust ajna chakra, the command center in the region of the forehead. As we have seen, this center corresponds to the space housing our brain, more precisely the cortical brain, which interacts with the world through the senses. The cortical brain also interacts with the body by using the nervous system to execute bodily functions. Further, it interacts with the primitive brain by consciously retrieving memories.

The more untrained, unfocused, dull, and undernourished this center and the parts of the brain corresponding to it, the less capacity we have to protect ourselves from sensory onslaught. Similarly, the weaker and duller this center, the stronger the influence exerted by the unconscious mind and the primitive brain on the part of the brain that executes our conscious behaviors and decisions. Therefore, the vitality, strength, stamina, clarity, and one-pointedness of this center are the foundation for attaining mastery over our thoughts, speech, actions, and reactions. Without mastery over this center we are caught in the storms arising from the objective world and the world made of our memories. We remain victims of the concerns pertaining to the past and future and have little or no ability to live in the present. That is why, in Vishoka Meditation, we first master this center, and thereafter, by using the resources we discover here, we launch all other quests and conquests.

We gain mastery over the center of the forehead by remaining focused on the combined forces of the breath and mind at this center for the 48 seconds required for the pair to bond with each other. In this 48-second interval we gain a direct experience of the inward flow of mind and the joy spontaneously emerging from it. This experience becomes our inner guru and source of inspiration. As practice continues and we are able to stay focused at the center of the forehead for longer than 48 seconds, our ability to face and conquer distractions and disturbances arising from both the inner and outer worlds increases. We are not perturbed by what we see and feel. We witness it and, if need be, examine its merits or demerits; otherwise, we simply let it go. When our concentration on the forehead center extends to approximately 9.6 minutes, our deep-rooted habits and addictive behaviors no longer have the power to distract our mind. This is true empowerment. The first objective of Vishoka Meditation is to acquire this highly empowered mind.

We nourish the mind and reclaim its original radiance and vibrancy by training the mind to stay focused on the concentrated pool of *prana shakti*, the life force, at the center of the forehead. Mind and breath are inseparable friends. They stay together and work together. Neither is static. They are ever-pulsating waves of consciousness.

In regard to these two inseparable, ever-vibrating, intelligent forces, focusing the mind is a twofold process: constant awareness of the movement of the breath, and confining that awareness in a well-defined space at the center of the forehead. Unless the mind is fully aware of the movement of the breath and is absorbed in this awareness, the mind and prana shakti flow on two separate tracks. This allows disturbances, distractions, inertia, and confusion to barge in. The mind is fully nourished and protected when it is united with the breath so profoundly that it has no awareness of anything other than the subtle movement of the breath. This constant awareness of the breath's sustained subtle movement is a state in which the mind is fully absorbed in the breath. This is the first step in the process of focusing the mind.

We accomplish this first step by paying attention to the movement of the breath at the opening of the nostrils, by paying attention to the joyful feeling at the inner corners of the eyes, and by paying attention to the inward flow of energy at the eyebrow center and to the upward lift of consciousness toward the center of the forehead. As this process matures, we become less and less aware of the physical dimension of the inhalation and exhalation and increasingly aware of the non-physical space corresponding to the part of our body above our throat, particularly the space in front of our face and forehead. Eventually, we are barely aware of the four distinct spaces corresponding to the opening of the nostrils, the inner corners of the eyes, the center between the eyebrows, and the center of the forehead— they have become a continuum. Our awareness is now focused on the space in front of our face and forehead.

The second step involves confining the mind, now fully absorbed in the breath, in the space corresponding to the center of the forehead. The mind is now absorbed in the ascending and descending waves of energy as we inhale and exhale. This absorption becomes so refined that the mind no longer feels its existence apart from the ascending and descending waves of energy and consciousness. At this point the union of mind and prana reaches maturity. We experience this fully matured union as pure pulsation, constantly rising and subsiding in the highly concentrated space in the center of the forehead.

Although the physicality of space vanishes in this state of consciousness, we may experience the pranic pulsation as if it were moving up and down. When we inhale, the mind follows the upward-moving pranic pulsation, and when we exhale, it follows the downward-moving pulsation. This upward and downward flow of awareness is extremely subtle—we hardly feel that we are breathing. Because from the very beginning of the practice—from aharana pranayama to samikarana pranayama, all the way through the main body of Vishoka Meditation—the mind and breath are engaged together, these twin forces undergo the process of refinement at the same pace. This is what empowers the mind to experience the upward- and downward-moving pranic current in the center of the forehead.

When this experience is maintained for more than 9.6 minutes, we have transcended the world of distractions, disturbances, concerns, and conflicts. We are absolutely at peace. This is the state of vishoka, an inner experience of joy untainted by any form of fear, doubt, sorrow, grief, or regret. When we return from this state, we bring with us the energy that is the antidote to fear, doubt, sorrow, grief, and regret.

Daily practice allows us to repeat this experience. Repeated experience fills our consciousness with the power to nullify our afflicting habits, thoughts, and emotions. In other words, this experience imbues us with the power to reclaim our pure and pristine self. As soon as we become reconnected with our pure and pristine self, the inherent power and wisdom of our body and mind return. The process of healing and rejuvenation accelerates. We are recharged with the energy we need to carry out our worldly pursuits and spiritual aspirations.

The Practice Step by Step

Create a space conducive to meditation. It should be clean, well ventilated, and softly lit. Keep this area as simple as possible. The fewer the objects in view, the less the chances of distraction. If you have an altar with a flame in your meditation room, sit with the flame directly in front of you. The mind has a natural tendency to go toward the source of light, even if your eyes are closed, so if the flame is positioned to the side, it will be difficult to maintain your focus in the center of your forehead.

Stability and comfort are the hallmarks of a meditative posture. You can adopt any of the classic sitting postures—such as lotus pose, accomplished pose, auspicious pose, and hero pose—as long as you are stable and comfortable, or you can simply sit cross-legged. If you have a problem in your knees or lower back, sit on a chair. If you sit on the floor, it is advisable to use a pillow to ensure your spine is straight and your knees rest on the ground. Comfort and steadiness are more important than an impressive-looking posture. You are comfortable and steady when your spine is straight, your shoulders are relaxed, and the weight of your torso is equally distributed on both buttocks.

Sit in a comfortable meditative pose with your head, neck, and trunk aligned. Withdraw your mind from all directions, and become aware of your body and the space it occupies.

Remind yourself that the time you have put aside for meditation is precious. Meditation is a time when you are with yourself in the present—not with your past or future. During meditation you are free from friends, foes, honor, insult, gain, and loss. You are free of your good and bad habits and your virtues and vices. Remind yourself that you were born without a specific identity, free of feelings of being rich or poor, beautiful or ugly. You were a carefree, innocent being. Feelings of shame and unworthiness were non-existent. Fear and anxiety couldn't touch you. You are meditating to restore your pure and pristine being. With this reminder, prepare yourself to do aharana pranayama.

Aharana

Pay attention to your breathing. Breathe gently, smoothly, and deeply. Do not exert yourself—stay within your normal capacity while you take five to seven smooth, deep breaths. There should be no noise or jerkiness in your breath.

When your body and nervous system are calm and quiet, bring your attention to the center of your forehead (which means bringing this center into your conscious awareness). Make sure that while attempting to focus at the center of the forehead you are not putting any strain on your eyes. Remain relaxed. Feel your presence at the center of your forehead and take three smooth, deep breaths.

Feeling your presence means you are aware only of your inhalation and exhalation. Because you are sitting comfortably with your head, neck, and trunk in a straight line, and your body and nervous system are completely at rest, with your diaphragm moving effortlessly, you have no awareness of the anatomical dimension of your breath. Your mind is free to feel the pranic counterpart of your breath at the center of the forehead. Breath and mind are fully united. While maintaining this state of awareness, take three smooth, deep breaths.

Now bring your attention to the center between the eyebrows and take one deep breath.

Next bring your attention to the eyes and take one complete breath.

Move on to your nostrils and again take one breath gently, smoothly, and silently. You are so deeply absorbed that you have no awareness of any part of the body other than the nostrils.

Next bring your attention to your throat, shoulders, upper arms, elbows, wrists, and palms, pausing at each of these points for the duration of one breath.

Then bring your attention to your fingertips and take two deep, relaxed breaths before moving back to your palms, wrists, elbows, upper arms, shoulders, throat, heart, bottom of the sternum, navel center, and pelvis, taking one deep breath at each of these points.

Then bring your attention to your perineum. Take two breaths here before moving back to your pelvis, navel center, bottom of the sternum, heart, throat, nostrils, eyes, eyebrow center, and center of the forehead, taking one breath at each place.

Finally, bring your attention to your crown center and take three breaths—enough to cultivate a significant degree of awareness here. Finish your final breath with an inhalation, and seamlessly slide into the next step of the practice, samikarana pranayama.

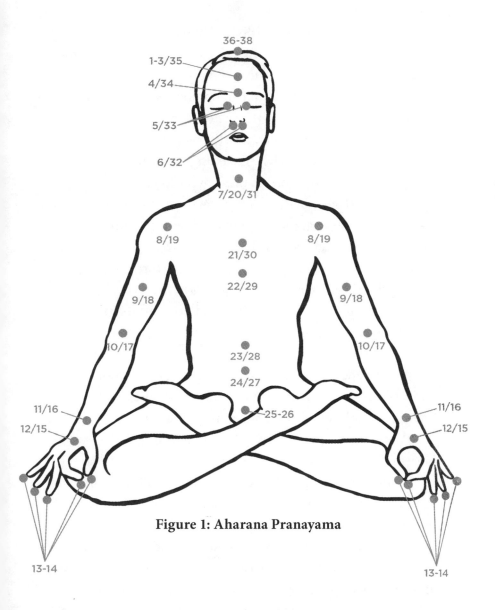

Figure 1: Aharana Pranayama

Samikarana

Samikarana pranayama is divided into two parts: descending breath and ascending breath. Exhaling, you allow the combined forces of your mind and breath to descend from your crown to the perineum while gently and smoothly sweeping through 8 distinct points in your body: the center of the forehead, eyebrow center, nostrils, throat center, heart center, bottom of the sternum, navel center, and pelvis. Including the crown of the head and the perineum, your breath thus covers 10 points.

You ended aharana pranayama with an inhalation at the crown center, so begin samikarana pranayama with an exhalation originating at the crown center. As you exhale, feel your breath descending from your crown, sweeping through your forehead, eyebrow center, nostrils, throat center, heart center, bottom of the sternum, navel center, pelvis, and down to the perineum. Without pausing at the perineum, begin inhaling and feel your breath flowing upward through the pelvis, navel center, bottom of the sternum, heart center, throat center, nostrils, eyebrow center, forehead center—and all the way to the crown. Repeat 10 times. The 10th breath completes samikarana pranayama.

While your mind follows the ascending and descending breaths between the crown and the perineum, it is important not to visualize these parts of your body. Simply allow your mind to feel the movement of the energetic dimension of your breath passing through these regions. In other words, pranic movement is the focal point of your awareness, not the body's anatomy. This allows the prana shakti to harmonize and nourish the organs and systems of the body that fall in its path. It also allows the mind to comprehend the field of energy and consciousness that naturally fills the body.

In other words, samikarana pranayama trains the mind to refine its comprehension and become aware of what lies beyond the physical level of existence. This acute comprehension empowers the mind to discover and transform the subtle causes of afflictions. The non-imaginary feeling of the upward and downward flow of awareness trains the mind for a successful inner quest.

Figure 2: Samikarana Pranayama

Vishoka Meditation

The main body of Vishoka Meditation begins after the 10 sweeping breaths of samikarana pranayama.

Samikarana ends with an inhalation into the crown center. Now, without pausing, begin exhaling, but this time do not descend all the way to your perineum. Instead, as you exhale, descend through your forehead, the center between the eyebrows, and the nostrils, and continue exhaling into the space extending 6–9 inches from the opening of your nostrils.

This process is extremely subtle. With practice you will cultivate a feeling for the depth of the space in front of your face and will be able to sense your breath moving into it. This is your personal space. It surrounds you like the atmosphere surrounds the earth. By sensing the extension of your exhalation beyond the nostrils, you are expanding the territory of your consciousness beyond the physical domain of your body and reclaiming the full range of your pranic field. In the beginning stages you may only be able to feel the flow of your breath an inch or so from your septum, but as you continue practicing, your sensitivity to the movement of breath will expand.

The first exhalation after samikarana pranayama is crucial. Pay attention to the subtlety of your exhalation, especially when you are trying to feel the flow of your breath beyond the physical structure of your nostrils. Do not visualize the space in front of your face. Space has no form, but it affords room for the breath to move. You are paying attention to the movement of the breath, not to the space. Cultivating sensitivity to the furthest frontier of your exhalation is one of the prime accomplishments in this system of meditation. The space corresponding to this furthest frontier is what we are calling the zero point.

Begin your inhalation at the zero point. Continue inhaling gently and smoothly. Feel the movement of your breath through the space in front of your face. Let your mind continue following the breath as it enters the nostrils and travels through the inner corners of the eyes, the center between the eyebrows, and all the way to the center of the forehead. The pace of your breath determines the pace at which your mind travels. Your inhalation terminates in the center of the forehead. Without pausing, begin exhaling and descend through the center between the eyebrows, the inner corners of the eyes, the nostrils, and all the way back to the zero point. Without pausing, begin inhaling from the zero point and go all the way to the center of your forehead. Descend again as you exhale. Do this 3–5 times.

As you continue practicing, you will notice the zero point moving further from your nostrils. This shift occurs in direct proportion to the refinement of your breath. With practice your breath becomes deeper, smoother, and so subtle that the physical sign of the breath's movement becomes almost undetectable. The subtler the breath, the more clearly and concretely the mind is able to identify the zero point. The less fuzzy the zero point, the more concrete the beginning point of Vishoka Meditation becomes. The concretization of the zero point makes us aware of the time it takes for the breath to travel through space before entering the nostrils. This awareness transforms the abstract understanding of the union of mind and breath into a living experience.

This experience enables the mind to identify the four distinct spots that fall in its path: the opening of the nostrils (the general region of the septum), the inner corners of the eyes (the medial canthi), the center between the eyebrows, and the center of the forehead. The mind becomes acutely aware of these four regions. This acute sensitivity empowers the mind to absorb the pranic elixir unique to each of those spots.

Awareness at the opening of the nostrils

After taking 3–5 breaths from the zero point to the center of the forehead, bring your attention to the opening of the nostrils, the first unique spot on the pathway of the united flow of mind and breath. Just as before, begin inhaling from the zero point. Continue inhaling through the space in front of your face, allowing your mind to register the instant your breath touches the opening of your nostrils: feel the spot the breath touches and the time when it touches. This awareness will enhance your mind's ability to be here and now.

This is an amazing experience. You are inhaling smoothly. At the beginning of your inhalation there is greater awareness of the zero point, the origination point of your breath. Within an instant, the septum and the space in its immediate vicinity become the center of your awareness. The movement of breath from the zero point to the opening of the nostrils remains part of your general awareness, but the focal point is the opening of the nostrils. Pay attention to when the incoming breath touches that exact spot, and let your mind continue moving along with the breath toward the center of the forehead.

The mind has a unique way of registering the experience that results when the united forces of mind and breath come into contact with the opening of the nostrils and the space corresponding to it. Yogis call this experience the joy of stillness (*sthira sukham*). The mind is grounded in the present. It is free from the distractions of past and future and is fully here and now. All mental faculties have come to a single focal point—the opening of the nostrils. This is mindfulness.

As you continue inhaling, your incoming breath passes through the opening of the nostrils, and as it does, it becomes charged with the joy of stillness unique to this spot. Continue inhaling, moving up through the nasal passage, the area corresponding to the inner corners of the eyes, the center between the eyebrows, and finally, the center of the forehead. This is where your inhalation terminates. Without pausing, begin exhaling. Descend with the exhalation, letting the united forces of your breath and mind move through the center between the eyebrows, the inner corners of the eyes, down through the nasal passage to the opening of the nostrils, and all the way to the zero point. Repeat this process 3–5 times, then move on to the next step.

Awareness at the inner corners of the eyes

Now the focal point of your awareness is the inner corners of the eyes. Just as before, begin your inhalation from the zero point, pass through the space in front of your face, and feel the touch of the incoming breath at your septum. Let your mind register the experience emerging from the contact of your breath with the septum. As you continue inhaling, the mind will carry the joy of stillness it has gathered here at the opening of the nostrils. However, this time as you are passing through the area of the inner corners of the eyes, pay attention to the feeling unique to this spot.

The experience here has a captivating quality that is characterized by sweetness (*madhu-mati*). Just as bees are drawn to sweet nectar (*madhu*), the mind is drawn to the nurturing nectar here. Just as you paid conscious attention to the spot at the opening of the nostrils in the previous step, now pay attention to the naturally occurring experience of sweetness in the region of the inner corners of the eyes. Let your mind register this experience.

Because the nature of this meditation demands that the breath and the mind travel together, the mind captures the experience of sweetness while it continues flowing upward in unison with the breath. The conscious awareness of the experience of sweetness unique to the inner corners of the eyes enriches the joy of stillness the mind has gathered at the opening of the nostrils. This frees the mind from the charms and temptations of worldly objects and concerns. After tasting this nectar, the mind loses its taste for objects it once found so alluring.

Remember not to make a mental effort to gather the nectar at the inner corners of the eyes. This is an effortless process—it happens by itself when the mind is still. This process is accomplished simply by making a mental note of it—anything more will create anxiety and disturb the smooth flow of your breath. As soon as the breath is disturbed, the mind is bound to be disturbed. Therefore, as you inhale, pass through this spot at the inner corners of the eyes while making a mental note of the unique experience, and continue inhaling. Pass through the center between the eyebrows and reach the center of the forehead, where the inhalation terminates and the exhalation begins. With the exhalation, travel through the center between the eyebrows, the inner corners of the eyes, the nasal passage, the opening of the nostrils, and all the way back to the zero point. Do this 3–5 times.

Awareness at the eyebrow center

Now your focus is the eyebrow center. The unique quality of the eyebrow center is upward movement (*urdhva-gati*). There is an amazing uplifting feeling at this center. As soon as the combined forces of mind and breath reach this spot, they are spontaneously pushed toward the center of the forehead.

The mind achieved freedom from the charms and temptations of worldly objects and concerns when it tasted the nectar at the inner corners of the eyes. Here at the eyebrow center it is infused with upward-moving energy. Riding the wave of upward-moving energy at this center is an extraordinary experience—one that enables the mind to discover the pranic counterpart of breath. It becomes clear that breath is more than an ingoing and outgoing movement of air. As soon as the mind becomes aware of this, it begins to draw life-sustaining energy from the primordial pool of prana shakti. The thrill of this realization gives the mind an uplifting feeling. Let the mind register it. You do not need to ask your mind to stay at this spot, nor do you need to ask it to quickly move on toward the center of the forehead. The intrinsic power of this center will push the mind upward. Simply let it happen.

Begin your inhalation at the zero point, keeping in mind that the center between the eyebrows is the focal point. Just as before, continue inhaling, passing through the opening of the nostrils, the inner corners of the eyes, the center between the eyebrows, and all the way to the center of the forehead. Without creating a pause, begin exhaling, passing back through all these points until you reach the zero point. Do this 3–5 times.

Awareness at the center of the forehead (ajna chakra)

You have reached the final step. Here the center of the forehead is the focal point. In the scriptures, this center is called *ajna chakra*, the command center. Using the energy unique to this center, the mind perceives the objective world, identifies and examines sensory experiences, and makes decisions. The inherent power of this center keeps the mind alert, assertive, and enthused. The distinctive quality of this center is inner light (*jyotishmati*). It is the light of intuition (*prajna*). Intuitive power is what makes humans so special. By using this power, the mind trains its faculties of logic and reason. With the help of this power, the mind figures out how to train the body, brain, nervous system, and senses to perform their functions. All cognitive functions fall in the domain of this center.

From a practical standpoint, this center is characterized by willpower, determination, courage, self-motivation, self-trust, inquisitiveness, and discernment. In every step of this practice, the combined forces of your mind and breath reach this center. In each of the steps leading to this final step, another spot—the opening of the nostrils, the inner corners of the eyes, or the eyebrow center—has been the focal point. By bringing those spots into your conscious awareness, the combined forces of your mind and breath discover, collect, and carry their unique energies to the center of the forehead. They bring the energy of stillness and comfort from the space corresponding to the opening of the nostrils, the energy of sweet joy from the inner corners of the eyes, and the upward-moving force from the eyebrow center.

Because the final step has the center of the forehead as its focus, the united forces of mind and breath descending from here will infuse the other three centers with the power unique to this center. As you ascend and descend between the zero point and the center of the forehead, the entire space and the unique energy centers located in it will become fully saturated with the feelings of stillness, non-sensory sweetness, upward movement, and intuitive awareness. Eventually, the distinct identities of these centers fade from the horizon of your consciousness.

You feel your breath only as a wave moving up and down in this pranically charged energy field.

In the beginning stages of this final step, you feel the presence of this energy field predominately in front of your face. You are aware of your face, your forehead, and your head, and at the same time, you are aware of the space in front of your face. But as the practice intensifies, the space becomes the locus for your consciousness, and your awareness pertaining to your physical self evaporates. By the time you have been absorbed in this practice for 5–7 minutes, the awareness of yourself as separate from the wave moving up and down in this pranically charged field begins to fade. You are this wave and this wave is you. In the scriptures, the experience of this wave is called *spanda*, the pulsation of pure consciousness.

The longer you stay in this state, the more your feeling of duality dissolves. You are pulled into the experience of oneness. This experience nullifies your deeply rooted afflictions of fear, doubt, sorrow, grief, and sense of unworthiness. You are free from your age-old loneliness, for you are fully connected with pure being. Your intuitive power returns. You are able to see the difference between what is essential and what is not. Past and future have no capacity to haunt you. You are living in the present and you are living fully.

This final step begins with an inhalation at the zero point. Let your mind flow along with the breath, passing through the opening of the nostrils, the inner corners of the eyes, the eyebrow center, and finally, the center of the forehead. By the time you reach the center of the forehead, your inhalation has reached its culmination point. Without pausing, begin exhaling and descend to the zero point.

The previous steps consisted of taking 3–5 breaths, but this step lasts longer. Do not count breaths. Just let the combined forces of your mind and breath go up and down from the zero point to the center of the forehead. Your goal is to stay with this step for 9–10 minutes.

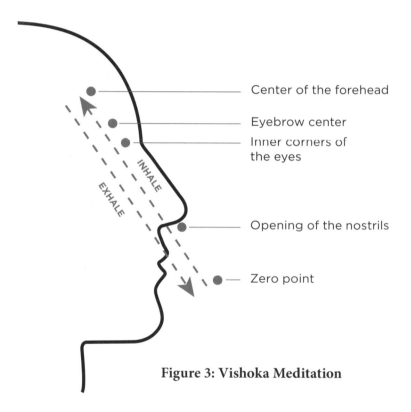

Figure 3: Vishoka Meditation

The Reward

When you have been absorbed in the practice for about five minutes, you experience a radical shift in your consciousness. You are barely aware of the physical dimension of your face and forehead; instead, you are becoming acutely aware of the space in front of your face. Similarly, you are barely aware of the physical dimension of breathing, but instead are becoming acutely aware of the energetic aspect of your breath.

As you continue inhaling and exhaling, you feel that the space in front of your face has become the locus of your consciousness. Subliminally, you feel the presence of this space in front of you, although a subtle feeling of its correlation with your face remains. As your practice deepens, your sensitivity to this space becomes stronger, until the entire region of your head is subsumed in it. The center of this pranically charged space becomes the center of your consciousness. Your sense of self-existence becomes concentrated here.

With each breath, you feel the wave of energy moving up and down. As it does, you feel as if the core of this space—the seat of your being—is bathing in this wave of energy. As your mental absorption in this wave intensifies, your cognition regarding this upward- and downward-moving energy becomes further refined. In this refined state of breathing you feel only the subtle movement of energy. The anatomical counterpart of breathing has disappeared. This is what is meant by "refinement."

The experience of your self-presence at the core of this space becomes concrete in proportion to the refinement of your breathing. At this stage in your practice, you are not witnessing the flow of your breath but are experiencing the pulsation of consciousness. This experience is not outside you—it is in you and *is* you. You are experiencing the timeless pulsation of yourself. There is no effort involved—it is happening by itself. The longer you maintain this awareness, the clearer, sharper, more luminous, and more discerning your mind becomes. The great master Patanjali calls this experience *vishoka* (*Yoga Sutra* 1:36), the state of mind free from afflicting tendencies of fear, doubt, sorrow, grief, and feelings of unworthiness. A mind free from these afflicting tendencies is your best friend. A mind afflicted with these tendencies is your worst enemy.

To reclaim and embrace your best friend, all you need to do is simply cultivate the capacity to maintain this last step of Vishoka for a minimum of 9–10 minutes. When you emerge from this 10-minute meditation, your highly potent, discerning, and benevolent mind comes with you. Driven by its inherent urge to discover and deliver lasting fulfillment and ultimate freedom, your mind will happily engage itself in worldly and spiritual endeavors in an orderly and highly productive manner. You no longer grope your way through the darkness of doubt, fear, uncertainty, and confusion. Past, present, and future have lost their power to haunt you. The wall that once separated the mundane from the sacred has fallen. You are a citizen of both worlds—the world within and the world without. You are equally at ease in both. This is freedom, the ground for lasting happiness.

CHAPTER 3
Laying the Foundation

Laying a solid foundation for meditation is as important as the practice itself. We all encounter obstacles in the course of our spiritual journey, but when our preparation is comprehensive and well thought out, we are able to overcome them more easily.

The *Yoga Sutra* tells us that in the course of our meditative quest we are likely to face one or more of the following obstacles: disease, mental inertia, doubt, carelessness, sloth, inability to withdraw from sense cravings, clinging to misunderstanding, inability to reach our goal, and inability to maintain the goal once it is achieved. Each of these obstacles causes pain, mental agitation, unsteadiness in our limbs and organs, and abnormal disturbances in our inhalation and exhalation. These painful conditions drain the vitality of our body and dull the brilliance of our mind. Attempting to meditate with a depleted body and a dull mind is a struggle. We must prepare ourselves for the practice of meditation by stopping the drainage of our vitality and brilliance, and by conserving our energy so we can invest it in a quality meditation.

The key preparatory steps can be divided into three categories: adopting a yogic lifestyle, preparing the body for a meditative pose, and cultivating healthy breathing.

Adopting a Yogic Lifestyle

Adopting a lifestyle conducive to living a full and healthy life is the most important step in preparing for Vishoka Meditation. Creating and embracing such a lifestyle requires understanding that we are a composite of body, breath, mind, and soul. When one facet is unhealthy, the others are bound to be unhealthy too. Improving the health of one of these facets automatically improves the health of the others.

People who are drawn to meditation for purely spiritual reasons cultivate virtues they believe will bring them freedom from the cycle of birth and death. In the process, they often ignore the importance of integrating the elements of meditation that ensure the health and well-being of the body, breath, and mind. On the other hand, people trained in modern psychology emphasize meditative techniques that calm and focus the mind, while those of a scientific bent regard meditation as a tool for stress management and emphasize the techniques that calm the brain and nervous system.

Seekers from all these various backgrounds fail to recognize the full scope of meditation. Its benefits stretch from the most mundane aspects of existence to the most sublime spiritual levels. This ancient system of meditation is built on the experiential wisdom of yogis and laymen alike, which holds that the body is the container of the mind and soul, and that the breath is the key to holding the body, mind, and soul in place.

Vishoka Meditation is built on integrating body, breath, mind, and soul. This system strongly recommends that we create an environment in which these four aspects of our being—body, breath, mind, and soul—are nurtured properly. Success in meditation is heavily dependent on a balanced way of living and being. This yogic lifestyle is a prerequisite for practicing meditation.

According to our tradition, five principles form the foundation of a yogic lifestyle: eating properly, exercising properly, engaging with the world properly, sleeping properly, and starting our day properly. The word used in the scriptures for "properly" is *yukta*, that which enables us to reconnect with our inner self. If well understood and put into practice skillfully, these five principles eliminate a large range of obstacles that disrupt our meditation. They ensure we do not encounter pain in our practice and we receive the full benefit of our meditation—vishoka, joy without a trace of sorrow.

Eating Properly

Poor health is one of the biggest obstacles in our personal quest. The principal cause is unhealthy eating habits, fueled by the modern way of life, which is extremely damaging to the innate wisdom of our body.

For thousands of years we ate only what nature provided. Our food was fresh and usually came from nearby. In these agrarian societies we had an opportunity to develop a personal relationship with the grains, fruits, vegetables, and dairy products we consumed. By contrast, today we hardly know what real food looks like. In our hypermobile, urbanized, industrialized, consumer-driven culture, the problems caused by chemically processed, manufactured food and unhealthy eating habits have reached epidemic proportions. Most of our food "grows" in factories and by the time it reaches our plates, its shape, texture, taste, fragrance, and color have been so drastically altered that the body has a hard time recognizing it.

To convince ourselves that these manufactured substances are food, we focus on the ingredients and nutrients listed on the package. Intellectually, this satisfies us that we are supplying our daily requirement of protein, carbohydrates, vitamins, and minerals, but the body instinctively asks, "Where is the actual food?" For example, the refined starches and concentrated sugars that are the hallmarks of chemically processed, industrialized food cause blood sugar to rise rapidly. It then falls below fasting levels within a few hours, causing hunger and leading to overeating. Conversely, whole fruits, vegetables, legumes, and minimally processed grains produce relatively small fluctuations in blood sugar, so the feeling of satiety lasts longer.

Eating properly does not need to be complex. It simply entails eating the right food, in the right proportion, at the right time, and with the right attitude. The right food is fresh, minimally processed, and genetically undisturbed. It is neither overcooked nor undercooked. It should be eaten in the right quantity—eating too much or too little is damaging.

Our attitude toward food is as important as its nutritional value. Food is the most visible and tangible conduit by which nature's finer forces nourish our body and mind. We establish and retain our connection with the life force through food. A respectful attitude toward food turns the process of eating into a spiritual ceremony. This creates a peaceful and positively charged environment both within and without. It calms our nervous system and awakens the endocrine system and digestive organs, balancing the rhythmic functions of our organs and the secretion and absorption of chemicals, hormones, and enzymes.

Exercising Properly

Exercising properly involves engaging in the right kind of exercise, in the right proportion, at the right time. Not all forms of exercise help us create physical and mental conditions conducive to meditation. A vigorous set of exercises may elevate our heart rate and burn calories, but if it does not make the body supple and relax the nervous system, it is of no use to a meditator. If a set of exercises does not clear the subtle energy pathways (*nadis*) and fails to awaken and energize the pranic centers hidden deep in our body, it is of limited value from the standpoint of meditation.

Proper exercise brings all the body's limbs, organs, and systems into a state of balance. Breath is the key. Even the yoga poses, popularly known as *asana*, help us build a solid foundation for meditation only when they enhance the quality of our breathing. The quality of our breathing is associated with the health of our lungs and heart, which in turn is closely related to the health of the navel center. Exercises that strengthen our abdominal cavity and restore the strength and rhythmic movement of our diaphragm are crucial. Such exercises calm our brain and nervous system—an internal condition that is a prerequisite for successful meditation.

Warm-up exercises and simple stretching, followed by classical yoga, are proper exercise. Additionally, yogis in the tradition of Vishoka Meditation highly recommend that we practice *agni sara* and *bhastrika pranayama* regularly. Agni sara energizes the entire abdominal region and consequently strengthens and optimizes the functions of all the organs located in the abdominal cavity. Bhastrika, on the other hand, strengthens and optimizes the function of our lungs. In the long run, it drives sloth and inertia from the body, restoring the mind's freshness and clarity. All of these practices—classical postures, agni sara, and bhastrika—are to be done in moderation.

Engaging with the World Properly

The third principle of a yogic lifestyle is engaging with the world properly. This requires familiarizing ourselves with the yoga philosophy of life. The main tenet of this philosophy is that to be born as a human is the greatest gift and to die without knowing the meaning of this gift is the greatest loss.

In light of this insight we learn to love and respect ourselves. We aspire to know about the reality that gave us the opportunity to be born as a human. We employ all our resources to know the essence of life and its creator. We are grateful to our family, friends, and the world. We love the world and work hard to give back more than we receive from it. Loving, giving, and making a difference become our nature, but at the same time we are fully aware that life is too precious to be consumed by worldly matters and relationships. It is a gift from a higher reality, it belongs to that reality, and we must use it to discover our relationship with that reality.

In the light of this awareness, we are able to enjoy worldly objects and relationships wisely and skillfully. We perform our actions lovingly and give credit to the higher reality that inspires and empowers us. This awareness transforms our worldview. We no longer see ourselves as doers but instead find ourselves to be instruments in the hands of higher reality. When we meet with the desired goal, we enjoy it with an attitude of surrender and gratitude. When we meet with failure, we do not despair.

In both cases, we maintain our equanimity—a requirement for a quality meditation.

Our actions are often propelled by our subtle tendencies—fear, anger, greed, ego, desire for revenge, hatred, jealousy, love, kindness, generosity, pity, and compassion. While acting under the influence of these impulses, we forget the precious nature of human birth and the transitory nature of worldly objects and relationships. We take worldly matters and relationships too seriously and become attached to our actions and their outcomes. The prospect of success and failure, loss and gain, honor and insult supplants our trust in life and its creator.

These pairs of opposites constantly churn our mind, causing it to lose its mastery over itself and the body. Such a mind has no capacity to calm itself at will. In other words, the more value we attribute to worldly objects and relationships, the stronger they become. We lose mastery over ourselves in the same proportion. Adopting this third principle—engaging with the world properly—is the antidote because it allows us to nurture an internal environment conducive to meditation.

Sleeping Properly

The fourth principle of a yogic lifestyle is sleeping properly. More than a third of our life is spent sleeping, yet we know very little about the dynamics of sleep or how to spend that time wisely and productively. Sleep is nature's way of helping us rest, relax, and rejuvenate our body and mind. When the sleep cycle is disrupted, the healing and nourishing effect of sleep is compromised.

The sleep cycle has several components, most notably deep sleep and dreaming. Deep sleep is characterized by the lack of awareness of everything, including the process of sleeping itself.

Upon awakening, we have no recollection of what transpired during sleep. Deep sleep has no content. If we are aware of anything, it means our sleep was punctuated by dreams.

Dreams are purposeful and therapeutic, provided their duration and content do not disturb the quality of our sleep. Dreaming all night is detrimental to our well-being, and nightmares, particularly recurring ones, are indicative of serious present and future health problems.

With the exception of supremely accomplished yogis, all of us go through a regular cycle of dreaming and deep sleep. The transition period from waking to the sleeping state is filled with dreams, and normally this first round of dreaming is short. Following a short reverie-like dream, we go into deep sleep. In the case of a healthy person, this lasts somewhere between 90 and 120 minutes. Then we switch back to the dreaming state, which also lasts from about 90 to 120 minutes. If the dream state lasts longer than this, and if the qualities of the dreams shake our brain and nervous system, make our breath erratic, and thus prevent us from entering a state of deep sleep, it means the internal states of our body and mind are in dire need of repair and rejuvenation.

It is natural for dreams to cause rapid eye movement (REM). Dreams leading to rapid eye movement are gentle (*mridu*) and therapeutic. Through such dreams, the mind revisits its unfulfilled thoughts, feelings, desires, and ambitions. It unwinds its past and reflects on old issues. By using the ingredients of the present, the dream resolves unfulfilled desires and past issues. It does this without draining the resources of the body, mind, and nervous system. But when our dream world is turned upside down by the stormy contents of the mind, our breath and nervous system are thrown into chaos. That is damaging. When we wake up from such dreams, we are exhausted. This fourth principle of the yogic lifestyle—sleeping properly—requires avoiding stormy dreams.

Adhering to the first three principles of the yogic lifestyle will do much to help us avoid stormy dreams and sleep deeply. A complicated and unresolved past is a major contributor to disturbing dreams, but the quality of our food and our eating habits are major suppliers of what this unresolved past needs to stir up our internal states. While we do not have easy access to our past, we do have all the tools and means to correct our eating habits and eat the right food, at the right time, in the right proportion, and with the right attitude. Committing ourselves to a methodical system of breathing and relaxation to calm our brain and nervous system is another key to restoring sound sleep.

According to the tradition, the most important and effective practice for calming and eventually nullifying the root cause of stormy dreams is mantra sadhana—a subject addressed in chapter 4.

Starting the Day Properly

Starting the morning properly sets the tone for the rest of the day. This is the fifth principle of a yogic lifestyle. When our need for sleep has been met, our primitive brain sends a signal to the cortical brain, which prepares the body to become aware of its surroundings. It is important to listen to our biological clock and get out of bed promptly. When we ignore it, we invite sloth, inertia, and laziness. Staying in bed after our biological alarm has awakened us results in useless dreams. Further, instinct has prepared the colon and bladder to get rid of waste matter promptly when we wake up, but lingering in bed prevents them from performing their duties, thereby disrupting the body's ecology.

The most visible sign that we are not beginning our day properly is the lack of a bowel movement shortly after rising. Prolonged constipation is uncomfortable and the breeding ground for a host of physical and psychosomatic diseases. In the context of meditation, lack of a timely and complete bowel movement is directly associated with a foggy mind and lack of motivation—the more clogged and heavy the colon, the more clogged and heavy the mind.

Summon your willpower and get out of bed at the first prompting from your biological alarm and resolve to attend nature's call within 30 minutes after waking. To assist yourself in keeping this resolution, wash your face and brush your teeth as soon as you get up, and then prepare hot lemon water or Indian-style chai with plenty of ginger and only a few tea leaves. Sip the hot liquid while sitting in *virasana*, the hero pose, or *sukhasana*, the easy pose. Form a habit of refraining from checking your texts, email, and social media feed in the first 30 minutes after you wake up. It takes only a few weeks to retrain the eliminative system to hear and heed the natural rhythm of the body. The outcome of this retraining is extremely rewarding.

It is also important to put aside 2–5 minutes during the first 30 minutes in the morning to reflect on the value of being born as a human and all the gifts that accompany human birth. Reflect on how quickly time flies and how important it is not to postpone your happiness. Remind yourself that happiness is your own creation. To find happiness, you must cultivate a clear, calm, and one-pointed mind. Because such a mind can be contained only in a healthy body, you must do everything in your power to acquire a healthy body. No wealth is superior to a healthy body and a peaceful mind. Remind yourself that the time-tested practice of Vishoka Meditation is the way to acquire this wealth. This sets the tone for the day, and you will find yourself looking forward to meditation as well as to what the rest of the day will bring.

Preparing the Body

The second step in laying the foundation for Vishoka Meditation is preparing the body to be comfortable in a meditative pose. Meditation is done in a seated posture. There are a variety of sitting poses: lotus pose (*padmasana*); accomplished pose (*siddhasana*); auspicious pose (*svastikasana*); hero pose (*virasana*); easy pose (*sukhasana*); and half lotus pose (*ardha padmasana*), to name a few.

Today the preferred meditative posture is sukhasana, the easy pose. Easy pose is a simple cross-legged posture. It creates the least amount of compression and tension in the feet, ankles, knees, thighs, sitting bones, and hips, and therefore causes the least discomfort. Whatever little discomfort it may cause in the lower back, hips, and knees can easily be removed by adjusting the height and shape of the cushion.

Finding Steadiness and Comfort

Steadiness and comfort are the hallmarks of a meditation posture. Instability and discomfort go hand in hand. An unstable and uncomfortable posture leads to pain and is a recipe for distraction. Pain can be overcome with relaxation techniques and a series of select postures that yogis have used for centuries.

Classical yoga postures, which make our body supple and energize our limbs and organs, help us overcome physical discomfort when we follow two golden rules. The first is to maintain effortlessness. We practice postures effortlessly by reaching the threshold of pain at the peak point of the posture, but never going beyond that threshold. Upon reaching that peak point, we relax and inhale and exhale as fully and effortlessly as possible. This allows connective tissue to stretch within its current capacity. We maintain this state of effortlessness for only 5–10 seconds before gently releasing the pose. Postures accompanied by the practice of effortlessness allow us to become aware of our threshold of pain; as blood circulation increases, nutrients are supplied to the affected tissues and the process of healing and nurturance accelerates. This way, regular practice of postures gradually removes our physical discomfort.

The second golden rule is to practice postures with the awareness of the space that fills every nook and cranny of our body and allow the mind to immerse itself in that space. Cultivating awareness of the space and cultivating this immersive state of mind is accomplished by practicing relaxation.

The 75-Breath Practice

There are numerous relaxation techniques. The one I find most helpful is known as the 75-breath practice, a technique passed on to me from the long line of Himalayan masters. This is one of the most significant practices for gaining self-mastery and is a prerequisite both for advanced practices of meditation and for the practices designed for gaining siddhis, extraordinary powers. It is a multistep practice, but in the context of Vishoka Meditation we apply only the first step. The purpose of this first step is to provide complete rest to our body, remove the pain caused by daily wear and tear, and enable us to become aware of—and eventually heal—tissue damage. There is no practice as effective as this for overcoming generalized chronic pain, relaxing the muscles, and calming the nervous system. This practice can be adopted as part of a daily routine and can be done at any time of day, provided we are not too full, too hungry, or too thirsty.

If the most convenient time to do this practice is just before meditation, take care to leave a gap of several minutes between completing it and beginning to meditate. Due to its deep, relaxing effect, this technique may lead to a pseudo-meditative state, which can easily be dominated by inertia, causing us to prefer remaining in this state to meditating. It is important to use this pain-free, pseudo-meditative state to engender a sense of freshness and awaken our peacefully energized mind. We accomplish this by concluding this practice at the 75th breath, then gently moving into a seated position and standing up before sitting for meditation.

This technique is essentially a combined practice of breathing (*pranayama*) and concentration (*dharana*). Its relaxing, healing, and energizing effect is largely dependent on the lack of effort involved. It entails taking 75 breaths following the standard rules of yogic breathing: breathe deeply, smoothly, slowly, and silently. Inhalation and exhalation follow each other seamlessly without pause.

We take 10 breaths from the toes to the crown and another 10 from the ankles to the crown. Then we take 5 breaths each from the knees to the crown, the perineum to the crown, the navel to the crown, the heart to the crown, the throat to the crown, and the center of the forehead to the crown. This constitutes 50 breaths. We then take 25 breaths from the opening of the nostrils to the center of the forehead.

Bear in mind that breathing between point A and point B

means bringing our awareness to point A at the beginning of the inhalation, reaching point B as we complete the inhalation, and reaching point A again as we complete the exhalation. This movement of awareness is fully coordinated with the movement of the breath. In other words, although the physical counterpart of the breath travels as air from the opening of the nostrils to the lungs, we mentally watch the subtle movement of energy between point A and point B as we breathe. During this process, the less aware we are of the physical counterpart of the breath—the air's movement—the more aware we are of the joint journey of our mind and the energetic counterpart of the breath. In effect, in this relaxation practice, we are meditating on the flow of consciousness from point A to point B.

For the first few days or weeks, we may not feel the movement of awareness between these points or we may feel the movement only at some of these points, such as between the opening of the nostrils and the forehead. Eventually, however, the mind becomes acutely aware of the movement of the subtle aspect of the breath, which allows the intrinsic power of the breath to awaken the body's inherent ability to heal and rejuvenate itself. Even long before the mind becomes fully aware of the incessant flow of the energetic dimension of the breath, the mind's engagement in going through the motion of the technique is deeply relaxing and energizing.

Find a clean, quiet place in which to do the 75-breath practice, because any loud or unexpected sound will jar the nervous system. This practice is always done while lying on the back, preferably on the floor. Make sure the floor is not cold and is cushioned with a yoga mat, rug, or thick blanket. Use a neck pillow just thick enough to fill the space between your neck and the floor. This will keep you free from tension caused by the weight of your head, allowing you to reach a deeper state of relaxation. As the practice progresses you may feel cold, so cover yourself with a light blanket. Make sure it is not too heavy because the weight will be distracting, especially in the area of your toes.

••••••••••••••

Begin the 75-breath practice by lying on your back. Position a pillow under your neck and cover yourself. Spread your legs so your feet are about nine inches apart. If your back or sacrum is stiff or if you find it uncomfortable to spread your legs fully, put a bolster or a rolled-up blanket under your knees. Your arms should be a comfortable distance from your body with your palms up and your fingers slightly curled.

Now bring your attention to your body. Feel the presence of yourself in your body. Take a couple of normal breaths. When your body is settled on the floor and the exertion created by placing the pillow under your neck and tucking yourself inside the blanket has subsided, bring your attention to your toes.

Begin inhaling, allowing your awareness to travel upward, passing through the ankles, knees, perineum, navel, heart, throat, and forehead, all the way to the crown. It is normal to have little or no feeling of upward movement when you are mentally passing through your legs, but it is important to make the attempt. A significant feeling of upward movement of awareness begins only when the united forces of mind and breath reach the abdominal region, particularly the navel center and beyond. Preserve your experience of upward movement in the navel area and use that memory during subsequent inhalations to kindle that same feeling in the space that stretches from your toes to the abdominal cavity. This will eventually enable your mind to pull the lower regions of your body into conscious awareness, and you will be able to feel a noticeable degree of movement of energy in that region. This allows the mind to reclaim ownership of the body.

Coordinate the movement of your mental awareness and the movement of your breath so that the upward movement of your awareness reaches the region of the crown exactly when your inhalation reaches its culmination—your mind and breath travel at the same pace.

As soon as the combined forces of the mind and breath reach the crown, begin exhaling. With the exhalation, the mind travels downward, passing through the forehead, throat, heart, navel, perineum, knees, and ankles, finally reaching the toes. This journey constitutes one breath. Without pausing, begin inhaling. Let your mind follow the trail of your breath, once again passing through all these points and reaching the crown at the end of the inhalation. Without a pause, begin to descend while exhaling. Repeat this eight more times for a total of 10 breaths. However, during the 10th exhalation do not go all the way to your toes, but stop at your ankles.

Without pausing, begin inhaling from your ankles and travel back to the crown. Then descend to the ankles again with the exhalation. Do this 10 times, but during the 10th exhalation, stop at the knees instead of exhaling all the way to your ankles.

Without pausing, begin your inhalation at your knees. Go all the way to the crown and descend with the exhalation. Do this only five times. With the fifth exhalation, stop at the perineum and begin inhaling from there, taking five breaths. Following this pattern, breathe five times between the navel and the crown, the heart and the crown, the throat and the crown and, finally, the center of the forehead and the crown.

At the fifth exhalation from the crown to the forehead the

pattern changes. This time, instead of stopping at the center of the forehead, continue exhaling to the opening of the nostrils. Then inhale from the opening of the nostrils to the forehead. Without pausing, descend with the exhalation to the opening of the nostrils. Take 25 breaths in this manner. This completes the practice of the 75-breath relaxation.

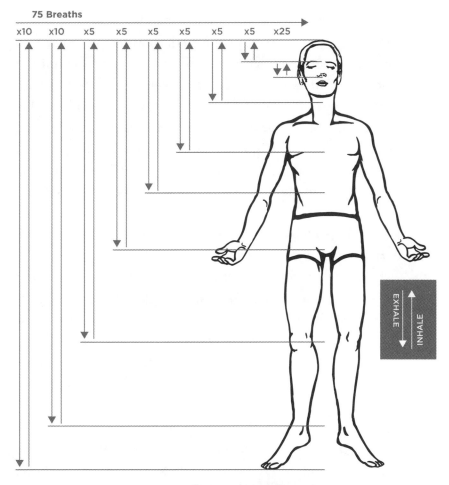

Figure 4: The 75-Breath Practice

The power of this practice to heal and transform lies in its simplicity. The seemingly incomprehensible and complex functions of our body are propelled and sustained by the force of pulsation (*prana*). This mysterious pulsating force gives birth to the body and mind—we exist because of it. Even though our life depends on this pulsation, most of the time we are oblivious of it.

The 75-breath practice enables our mind to cultivate a conscious awareness of this force. This awareness transforms the relationship between the mind and the force behind the pulsation of life. The more cognizant our mind is of this relationship, the more effortlessly its dormant forces awaken. This awakening leads to the manifestation of willpower, endurance, fortitude, and determination. The mind becomes charged with renewed vigor and enthusiasm. It regains confidence that it is the master of matter—the body. The rest of the inner quest begins from here. It may take time for the mind to achieve this level of mastery, but even in the beginning stages the process is deeply rewarding.

There are a few pieces of practical advice to keep in mind when doing this practice. The first has to do with counting your breaths. For the first few days, you may find counting to be a distraction. Very soon, however, you mind will summon its power of intention and come to know those numbers without counting. It is important to trust your mind when this happens. Your sixth sense will become your guide.

You will notice the length of your breath expands during this practice. In the normal course of life, you take somewhere between 15 and 20 breaths per minute. During this practice, you will be taking between 8 and 12 breaths per minute. Your breathing will further slow to between 5 and 8 breaths per minute if you are free from the anxiety of counting your breaths, if your spine is fully flat on the floor, if you are not using a cushion under your knees, and if the left and right sides of your body are perfectly aligned. Do not mistake this slow breath for shallow breathing. It is a deep and profound breath. At this breathing rate, your nervous system and visceral organs, especially the heart and lungs, are fully at rest. This accelerates the process of healing and repair.

It is common to fall asleep during this practice. The more tired and depleted you are, the greater your chances of falling asleep. Use your willpower to avoid this. The rejuvenating effect of completing the practice without falling asleep far exceeds the quality of rest provided by three hours of normal sleep. If you do fall asleep and remain asleep for more than 20 minutes, discontinue the session and resume the practice the next day. If you have dozed off only briefly, you may resume the practice at the point where you dozed off. But remember, if you fall asleep for a relatively longer stretch, do not resume the practice until the next day.

A final word of advice: Do not begin your meditation while you are still in this relaxation pose. It is tempting to remain in your relaxation pose after you have finished the practice, and it is even more tempting to simply begin meditating while still lying on the floor. This is unhealthy and should be avoided. Meditating in a relaxation pose as an extension of the 75-breath practice can make you lethargic and may have a negative effect on your muscle tone. Transform the deeply relaxed state of your body and nervous system into a fresh and energetic state by rolling onto your left side and gently getting up.

Cultivating Healthy Breathing

The third preparatory step for Vishoka Meditation is the cultivation of a healthy breath. Healthy breathing is the key to successful meditation. A healthy breath allows us to enter a state of deep meditation with minimum effort. If our breathing is unhealthy, we waste time fighting with our body and mind, and have neither time nor energy for meditation itself.

Cultivating healthy breathing is also essential to restoring overall health and a sense of well-being. Healthy breathing is measured by its smooth, effortless, and silent flow; unhealthy breathing is shaky, labored, and noisy. A noticeable pause between breaths is a further indicator of an unhealthy breath. The less perceptible the pause, the healthier we are.

The process of breathing is simple and extremely subtle. It runs on autopilot—the impulse behind breathing is beyond the realm of conscious awareness. Throughout our life, the breath flows incessantly and effortlessly. The life-giving and life-sustaining mystery of breath lies in this incessant and effortless flow. As soon as the breath becomes choppy and labored, life becomes burdensome. The longer the pause between breaths and the more effort involved in breathing, the foggier and more disoriented the mind.

The physiological component of breathing is simple. As our diaphragm moves upward our lungs contract, causing them to expel air, and we exhale. As the diaphragm descends, the lungs expand, drawing air in, and we inhale. The movement of the diaphragm and the function of our lungs are regulated by the autonomic nervous system, more precisely by the vagus nerve.

As long as the function of the autonomic nervous system

is balanced, the diaphragm moves freely. The smooth, rhythmic movement of the diaphragm allows the lungs to contract and expand. The unrestricted contraction and expansion of the lungs allows us to breathe effortlessly. But as soon as the function of our autonomic nervous system is disrupted, the movement of the diaphragm is constrained, the lungs are strained, and the breath becomes erratic, shaky, noisy, shallow, and labored. Under such conditions, we tend to hold our breath unconsciously and against our innate impulse. If this pattern continues, we form a habit of unhealthy breathing, and the consequence is a depleted body and a scattered mind.

Restoring healthy breathing begins with re-establishing the rhythmic movement of the diaphragm. The diaphragm is the part of the body most actively involved in the breathing process. Its movement propels the function of the lungs.

The problem is that we have become accustomed to sitting positions that restrict the movement of the diaphragm. When we sink into couches, chairs, and car seats, we reduce the space in the abdominal area and restrict the movement of the diaphragm; this in turn reduces the contraction and expansion of the lungs. The volume of our inhalation and exhalation declines while our demand for oxygen remains the same. To meet this demand, we resort to chest breathing, which stresses our lungs, heart, and liver, because a third or more of the lower lung has no chance to expand. Chest breathing is one of the leading causes of stress and chronic fatigue.

The remedy lies in re-establishing diaphragmatic breathing. This is a two-part process: restoring the diaphragm's rhythmic movement and restoring its natural strength and stamina.

Restoring the Rhythmic Movement
of the Diaphragm

The crocodile pose (*makarasana*) is one of the best ways to restore the diaphragm's rhythmic movement. To practice this pose, lie on your abdomen. Fold your arms and rest your forehead on your forearms or the back of your hands. This elevates your torso, allowing your abdomen to rest fully on the floor.

Breathe as gently and deeply as possible. As you inhale, observe how your abdomen presses against the floor while simultaneously expanding upward and sideways. As you exhale, observe how your abdominal region relaxes, allowing the entire abdomen to flatten against the floor. Take 10 breaths in this manner.

Figure 5: Crocodile Pose

The secret of the crocodile pose is that it allows us to observe the movement of the diaphragm. The elevated position of the chest lengthens the lower torso, creating more space in the abdominal region. The weight of the torso is compressing the abdomen, but the diaphragm is free to move up and down. This gives the mind the opportunity to consciously observe the movement of the diaphragm. The conscious awareness of this process trains the diaphragm to comply with the commands of the autonomic nervous system. As soon as the diaphragm resumes its full function, the habit of chest breathing disappears and we are able to breathe effortlessly.

Restoring the Natural Strength of the Diaphragm

The diaphragm is one of the strongest muscles in the body. It falls in the domain of the solar plexus, an energetic field technically known as *rudra kuta*, the peak (*kuta*) of the life force (*rudra*). The solar plexus corresponds to the region from the perineum to the sternum. From the standpoint of breathing, the diaphragm is the most significant muscle in this energy field. In yoga mythology, Rudra is the most valiant, radiant, and energetic god. At the muscular level, the diaphragm embodies all these qualities.

When we work to strengthen the diaphragm, we automatically strengthen and energize the muscles, ligaments, and tendons directly or indirectly connected to it. That in turn leads to the strengthening of all the organs located in the abdominal cavity. One of the easiest and most efficient ways of strengthening the diaphragm and abdominal region is to breathe with weight on the abdomen. Because for centuries yogis have used bags of sand for this purpose, we call it sandbag breathing.

••••••••••••

To practice sandbag breathing, lie on your back with a properly sealed bag of sand on your abdomen. In the beginning a 5-pound bag will be sufficient. The sand should be malleable enough to mold itself to the shape of your stomach. Make sure that the bag is not resting on any portion of your rib cage.

Relax and breathe. You will notice the inhalation requires some effort, but during the exhalation the weight pushes your abdomen down, and the air is expelled from your lungs effortlessly.

If the effort involved during the inhalation makes you uncomfortable, it is an indication that the natural strength and stamina of your diaphragm have declined significantly. If you are unable to relax and exhale completely and effortlessly, it means not only that your diaphragm is weak but also that the energetic field of your solar plexus and corresponding organs is in poor health. In either situation, reduce the weight.

Work with this practice for 5–7 minutes. Then remove the sandbag and enjoy a few relaxed breaths without the sandbag.

Figure 6: Sandbag Breathing

The secret of sandbag breathing lies in your ability to observe your exhalation and the unique feeling of lightness induced by it. This feeling is an indication that the weight of the sandbag is helping you exhale more deeply and more effortlessly, triggering your relaxation response. As your tension and stress melt away, you feel a sense of lightness.

An urge to lengthen your exhalation is an indication that your diaphragm has become stronger and you can add more weight. By the time you have cultivated the capacity to breathe comfortably with a 12-pound weight, you will have acquired a strong diaphragm and overcome the habit of chest breathing.

When you are able to enjoy sandbag breathing with a 16-pound weight, you will have fully reclaimed the innate strength of your abdomen, a condition that supports healthy breathing.

Purifying the Energy Channels

The physical frame of the body is supported by a non-physical, energetic counterpart known as the *pranamaya kosha*, the pranic sheath. It comprises numberless energy channels called *nadis*. Yogis have identified and studied 72,000 nadis. From the standpoint of meditation, 14 nadis stand out. Among these, the three most important are *ida*, *pingala*, and *sushumna*. Ida and pingala are respectively associated with lunar and solar, passive and active, and feminine and masculine energies. The perfectly balanced state of these two is sushumna.

Every part of the body is associated with the mutually supporting forces of ida, pingala, and sushumna, and these forces carry out every physiological function. The breath flowing through the left nostril carries the properties of ida (lunar or feminine energy), whereas the breath flowing through the right nostril carries the properties of pingala (solar or masculine energy). One nostril is usually more dominant, which means more air flows from that nostril. Left or right nostril dominance is the most tangible function of the lunar and solar energy channels. This dominance is a reflection of the internal state of our body and mind.

When our left nostril is dominant, we tend to be passive, lethargic, and despondent. In contrast, when our right nostril is dominant, we are more prone to be active, energetic, and aggressive. The dominance of the left nostril supports the function of the parasympathetic nervous system; the dominance of the right nostril supports the sympathetic nervous system. However, because of the incessant rise and fall of microcycles of ida, pingala, and sushumna dominance, our moods, behaviors, emotions, and biological functions do not manifest in the distinct black-and-white fashion described above. These microcycles are brief and so subtle as to be perceptible only to yogis with highly trained minds.

Macrocycles, however, are observable. They last somewhere between 90 and 120 minutes and are inherent in our normal experience. For example, the breath flows more predominately through the left nostril for about 90 minutes before switching to the right nostril. In another 90 minutes or so, it switches back to the left nostril. In between, there is a period of transition lasting from a few seconds to a few minutes. At this time sushumna, the central energy channel, is dominant and the left and right, lunar and solar, feminine and masculine energies are perfectly balanced. When sushumna is dominant, we are neither active nor passive, aggressive nor despondent, but clear and peaceful. This state leads neither to action nor to inaction but to self-awareness. In other words, it is devoid of all content, both positive and negative.

These macrocycles of nostril dominance have a significant effect on our well-being. When we continually breathe predominantly through one nostril, the functions of our nervous system and internal organs become unbalanced, disrupting the body's ecology. For example, when the left nostril is dominant for more than two hours at a time, we are prone to be passive, lethargic, and unmotivated. When we breathe mainly through the right nostril for an extended period, we tend to be energetic and aggressive. In either case, our metabolism becomes imbalanced. For example, prolonged left-nostril dominance will slow our digestion while prolonged right-nostril dominance will accelerate it. Both of these conditions will have a negative effect on our mind, rendering it unfit for meditation. To fix this problem, yogis prescribe a unique pranayama practice known as *nadi shodhana*.

Nadi shodhana means "purification of the energy channels." When the tendency to breathe primarily through one particular nostril becomes habitual, the internal ecology of the body becomes lopsided, and the energy channels become either sluggish or hyperactive. The capacity of sluggish or hyperactive energy channels to process and eliminate physical toxins and mental impurities is compromised. Nadi shodhana eliminates impurities by allowing an equal amount of air to flow through each nostril; hence it is called channel purification.

This technique is also known as alternate nostril breathing, because its salient feature is breathing alternately through one nostril at a time, in a carefully measured and controlled manner.

There are several variations of nadi shodhana. The following variation is the least complicated and thus is easy to practice.

••••••••••••••

Assume your preferred sitting posture, making sure your head, neck, and trunk are aligned. Take a few normal breaths through both nostrils. When your breath is settled and your mind composed, take your last normal breath, ending with an inhalation.

Use your fingers to close your left nostril and exhale through the right. As soon as you finish exhaling, close the right nostril and inhale through the left. Without pausing, close the left nostril and exhale through the right. At the end of the exhalation, close the right nostril and inhale through the left. Then close your left nostril and exhale through the right.

At the end of the third exhalation through the right nostril, without pausing begin inhaling through that nostril. At the end of the inhalation, close the right nostril and exhale through the left. Following this pattern, exhale through the left nostril three times.

At the end of the third exhalation through your left nostril, begin inhaling through that same nostril without pausing. At the end of the inhalation, close your left nostril and exhale through the right. Continue until you have exhaled through the right nostril three times. After finishing the third exhalation through the right nostril, resume breathing through both nostrils. This constitutes one round of alternate nostril breathing.

One round of the practice has three parts: in the first part, you exhale three times through the right nostril; in the second part, you exhale three times through the left nostril; in the third part, you again exhale three times through the right nostril. Thus, you have exhaled six times through the right nostril and only three times through the left. To balance the number of exhalations in the two nostrils, you must do a second round. During this round, you begin exhaling with the left nostril, in contrast with the first round, when you began with the right nostril.

When you have completed these two rounds, you will have taken the same number of inhalations and exhalations through each nostril. For this reason you must always do two, four, or six rounds of alternate nostril breathing, never one, three, or five rounds.

The benefit you derive from this practice is greatly dependent on your ability to breathe deeply and smoothly without creating a pause between breaths. A deep and smooth breath is dependent on the strength and rhythmic movement of the diaphragm, which are enhanced by the practices of sandbag breathing and

Figure 7: Nadi Shodhana

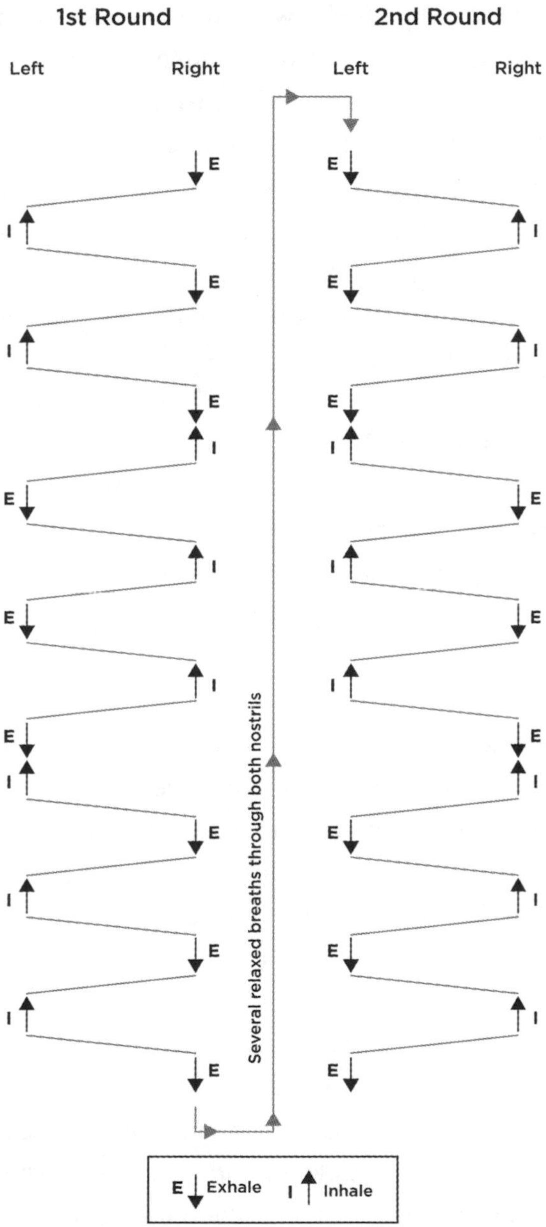

1st Round   **2nd Round**

Left   Right   Left   Right

Several relaxed breaths through both nostrils

E ↓ Exhale   I ↑ Inhale

diaphragmatic breathing in the crocodile pose. But the problem associated with the pause between breaths is subtler and more potent, for it stems from afflicting tendencies, such as fear, aversion, attachment, confusion, and a misplaced sense of self-identity hidden in the depths of the mind. The practices that restore the strength and rhythmic movement of the diaphragm help us solve only the physical conditions contributing to the pause between breaths. The subtle causes hidden deep in our mind require a more subtle and potent solution—*shvasa-prashvasa pravahi pranayama.*

Eliminating the Pause

Shvasa-prashvasa pravahi means "a technique that allows the inhalation and exhalation to flow seamlessly." This pranayama practice is measured and monitored by the sound *so hum*, so it is also called *so hum pranayama*. In some yoga traditions, it is taught as meditation due to its calming effect.

••••••••••••

To practice this technique, assume a comfortable sitting pose. Close your eyes. Mentally check the position of your spine to ensure your head, neck, and trunk are aligned. Withdraw your mind from all worldly objects and concerns. Become aware of your body and the space occupied by it. Mentally draw a circle of light around yourself. Inside this circle of light, you are free and fully protected. Now, without putting any strain on your eyes, feel your own presence in the region of your forehead. Take a couple of normal breaths and let this feeling of self-presence fill the space in front of your face and all around your head.

Take three breaths. As you inhale, feel the touch of cool air at the opening of your nostrils. As you exhale, feel the touch of warm air. Your breath is relaxed. You are breathing deeply and smoothly, without a trace of noise or shakiness.

Now recall the sound *so hum*. This sound has two parts: *so* and *hum*. Coordinate the sound *so* with your inhalation and the sound *hum* with your exhalation. As you are inhaling, you are listening to the sound *so*, and while you are exhaling, you are listening to the sound *hum*. Continue your practice for about five minutes.

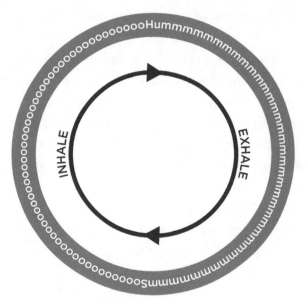

Figure 8: So Hum Pranayama

There are three points to note: First, listen to the sounds mentally but do not articulate them. Second, on the inhalation, lengthen the *o* at the end of *so*, and on the exhalation, lengthen the nasal sound at the end of *hum*. In other words, continue hearing *soooooooooo* all the way to the culmination point of your inhalation; without pausing, begin hearing *hummmmm* and continue listening to it all the way to the culmination point of your exhalation. *So* and your inhalation and *hum* and your exhalation are a single stream of awareness. Third, the gap between *so* and *hum* is almost non-existent. *Hum* begins at the tail end of *so,* and *so* begins at the tail end of *hum.* The end of one is the starting point of the other. This removes the pause that normally exists between inhalation and exhalation and between exhalation and inhalation. In other words, the sound *so hum* and the breath become an inseparable stream of awareness, and this awareness begins to flow seamlessly.

There is no set rule about how much or for how many weeks or months we should work with these four practices for cultivating healthy breathing: crocodile pose to restore the rhythmic movement of the diaphragm; sandbag breathing to restore the diaphragm's natural strength; alternate nostril breathing to purify the energy channels; and *so hum* breathing to eliminate the pause. Those who have adopted a yogic lifestyle and are consistent with the 75-breath relaxation practice may not need any of these ancillary practices, while people who have not yet developed healthy patterns may wish to practice some or all of these techniques.

CHAPTER 4

Optimizing Your Practice

Meditation is an inward journey—the mind's journey from the complex reality of the physical world to the simple, undistorted world of consciousness. Along the way, we use the power of breath to free the mind from its troublesome relationship with the external world and turn it toward the center of consciousness. This journey unfolds in several stages, each characterized by a unique experience, and culminates in samadhi.

Samadhi is absolute peace. In this state, we are established in our essential nature—pure, unbound, timeless, unborn, undying consciousness. To achieve this state, we must meditate regularly and sincerely. But as we shall see, the lives of great masters demonstrate that technique-driven meditation is only half of the practice. The remaining half consists of contemplative practices designed to help us maintain constant awareness regarding life's purpose and the role of meditation in achieving it.

The technique-driven aspect of meditation helps us form new, healthy habits, weaken unhealthy ones, relax our nervous system, gain mental clarity, and improve concentration. But it does not give us access to the deep-rooted tendencies that impede our progress nor enable us to confront these obstacles and overcome them. The contemplative aspect of meditation enables us to examine our core strengths and our core weaknesses. It enables us to cultivate trust in our strength, and gives us courage to discover and finally eliminate the root cause of our self-defeating tendencies.

The Danger of Invisible Obstacles: A Story of Narada

A story of Narada, the sage we met in the first chapter, will illustrate the problems that arise when we fail to see and address our deep-rooted tendencies.

Narada is one of the renowned *deva rishis*, celestial sages. Untouched by old age, disease, and death, he has access to every realm of creation—earth, heaven, and the space in between. All the *siddhis*, extraordinary abilities, are at his disposal. In complicated situations, even the gods, goddesses, and nature's finer forces seek his guidance and assistance. But before he reached this exalted state he was an ordinary person just like you and me.

Narada was orphaned at the age of five. He was raised by a group of sadhus, who taught him the principles of yoga and other spiritual sciences. Narada's love for knowledge and his sincerity in his practice won the favor of many masters. His intense and prolonged practice eventually drew the attention of Vishnu, who bestowed his guiding grace by adopting Narada as his student.

Having the good fortune to study and practice under the guidance of an exalted celestial being brought Narada instant freedom from all doubts and fears. He committed himself whole-heartedly to an intense practice. One by one, yogic powers began to manifest. Hunger and thirst no longer bothered him. His energy was inexhaustible and his mind crystal clear. He could bilocate at will. At some point in his yogic quest, he attained *kaya siddhi*, the power that makes a body indestructible. He could walk through solid walls and pierce an atom. He could travel in all three temporal realms—past, present, and future. These extraordinary powers led him to believe he had unraveled all the mysteries of the universe, including the mystery of his own mind.

Vishnu warned Narada about the tricky nature of the mind and advised him to examine the subtle impressions of his unfulfilled desires. He explained the powerful and mysterious nature of the mind and why even highly accomplished masters must practice introspection and self-inquiry. Vishnu stressed that on the path of self-conquest, ongoing self-assessment is an absolute necessity, and it should be done with complete openness, courage, and trustful surrender.

But the more Vishnu emphasized the importance of surveying the mind's landscape and discovering its hidden contents, the more Narada was convinced his master was being overcautious. Vishnu knew how painful it is to fall into the whirlpool of afflicting tendencies whose existence one has been denying. But he also knew falling into that whirlpool is the surest means of transcending these afflictions and, further, that Narada would soon encounter circumstances that would pull him into that vortex.

As instructed by Vishnu, Narada set out on an extended pilgrimage. Passing through the capital of a king known for his generosity, piety, and respect for spiritual seekers, he stopped at the palace gate. Hearing of the arrival of a highly dignified adept, the king came out to greet him and pay his respects. The king then asked Narada to stay at the palace and bless his family, an invitation the sage readily accepted.

The king knew that in addition to his spiritual wisdom, Narada was also an expert in astrology and palmistry, so in due course he asked the sage to read his daughter's palm and forecast her future. The princess had just reached adulthood and was very beautiful. Although the king and his council had presented the princess with the most handsome and qualified men in the kingdom as prospective husbands, she had rejected them all. All the courtiers were worried about her future and hoped Narada would find a solution.

When Narada agreed to help, the princess came to the assembly hall with her retinue. At her father's request, she extended her open palm to Narada. The instant Narada took her hand, an overpowering thrill ran through his body. The joy of touching her outshone even the joy he had experienced in samadhi.

Summoning his composure, he read her palm. "She is as beautiful as the goddess Lakshmi, and her inner beauty and richness are also equal to Lakshmi's," he announced to the assembly. "She is destined to have the greatest of all fortunes. She will marry a man equal to Vishnu in beauty, wisdom, and valor."

Then turning to address the king, Narada said, "O King, invite men from throughout the land to attend a *svayamvara* (a ceremony in which a woman chooses her own husband)."

The king readily agreed and left the hall delighted and reassured. Narada, however, walked away with a mind engrossed in thoughts of the princess. He wanted one thing and one thing only—to have this enchanting woman as his wife. He knew it would be almost impossible to win her hand in marriage, for he was neither royal nor rich nor handsome, but he also knew nothing was impossible for his master.

"Vishnu is omniscient and omnipotent," Narada mused. "He is supremely alluring and his love for me is limitless. He never disappoints me. He will definitely fulfill my desires."

Narada abandoned the rest of his pilgrimage, returned immediately to Vishnu, and placed his wish at his feet. Vishnu granted it, saying, "Anything that is mine is yours. My joy comes from seeing you happy."

Instantly, Narada saw himself as beautiful and youthful as Vishnu. He was confident that the princess would choose him over all other suitors. On the day of the ceremony, Narada joined the throng of would-be grooms. All were seated in identical chairs around the perimeter of a large hall. It was painful for Narada to sit on a chair no better than the chairs of those who did not have even a fraction of the beauty and dignity he possessed.

Holding a garland, the princess entered the hall accompanied by her retinue. She glanced around the room and began walking along the row of suitors, passing many men before she came to Narada. She paused in front of him and, smiling, gazed at him intently for a moment. Then she walked on. Narada could not believe it. The princess had passed him by! He was devastated. What was wrong with her? What could she be looking for that he lacked?

A little farther around the hall, the princess stopped in front of a man Narada had not noticed—Vishnu himself. She offered him the garland and he accepted. While everyone was cheering, Narada stormed out of the hall.

As he rushed away in a blind fury, he was caught up in an intense internal dialogue: "How could my master compete with his own student? Everyone in the world regards him as a god, the protector and provider. Is this how he protects and provides for the one he claims to love the most? And what to make of a woman who possesses such poor judgment? I have lost everything! Where should I go? What should I do?"

While tangled in these thoughts, Narada happened upon a lake. Stooping down to drink, he saw his reflection in the water. He had the face of a monkey! Now his anger truly had no limit. He decided to confront Vishnu at once and settle the score.

But Vishnu was no longer simply his guru and guide—he was the son-in-law of the king and heir to the throne. It took months for Narada to be granted an audience. When he finally found himself face-to-face with his master, Narada lost his temper. He summoned the powers of his austerities and the fruits of his yogic disciplines and concentrated them in a few drops of water resting on his palms. Hurling the water at Vishnu, he uttered a curse: "May you suffer from being deprived of a wife just as I am suffering now. May your wife be abducted by your enemy and may people like me, with the face of a monkey, come to your aid and help you reunite with your wife."

Vishnu accepted the curse calmly: "I desire nothing less than the best for you, even if it means becoming caught in the torrent of samsara."

How this curse eventually manifested when Vishnu incarnated as Rama is another story, but the calmness Vishnu exhibited when he was being cursed and the wisdom emitted by his words helped Narada recognize the subtle and potent tendencies he had been consistently denying he possessed.

Narada was an accomplished master with extraordinary powers. His words had such an unfailing effect that even a celestial being like Vishnu could not nullify them. And yet Narada had not been able to unravel the mystery of his own mind. During his formative years, he had heard that worldly relationships are the source of bondage and monasticism is the only way to liberation. The monastic life demanded that he renounce his desires, so he committed himself to intense practices without taking an inventory of his subtle mental tendencies.

His burning desire to become perfect was a clear sign that he was not perfect, and he knew it. But he did not know—and avoided knowing—where and how he was imperfect. As a monk he was practicing renunciation and non-possessiveness without a clear understanding of what he was trying to renounce and whether or not he was capable of doing so. He had a desire for a relationship. He had a craving for sensory pleasure and the fulfillment that comes from it, but he had been denying that he had any such feelings. The result? In an environment conducive to their awakening, these feelings exploded into manifestation, and even a great master like Narada could not resist them.

We need to understand and honor our deep-rooted tendencies. Rather than live in denial, we must make an effort to recognize our *prakriti*, the building blocks of our personality. As humans we are a unique blend of divine and beastly, good and bad, perfection and imperfection. We are a combination of positive and negative tendencies. We are made of both creative and destructive forces. It is important to recognize and cultivate our higher qualities, but it is equally important to recognize our lower qualities and try to minimize and eventually eliminate them. Recognizing, attenuating, and eliminating our lower qualities requires more wisdom, determination, and skill than recognizing and cultivating the higher ones. Cultivating the higher qualities is accomplished through technique-driven meditation, but recognizing, attenuating, and eliminating the lower qualities happens through the contemplative dimension of meditation.

The Transforming Power of Contemplation: The Story of Buddha

The following story demonstrates the transforming power of the contemplative aspect of meditation. Buddha was born a prince. In early childhood a renowned master, Asita, predicted that he would grow up to become either the greatest ruler in the land or the greatest spiritual master and leader the world had ever known. His father wanted his son to become the greatest king, so he made sure the prince lived in an environment devoid of all vestiges of spirituality. The king commissioned the best teachers to instruct his son in worldly matters: history, economics, politics, mathematics, dance, music, archery, horsemanship, and the science of warfare. Men and women specializing in *kama shastra*, the art of sensory pleasure, were employed to engage Buddha in a wide range of worldly pleasures early in life. Anyone who was sick or old was kept out of sight. Conversation containing even a trace of sorrow or grief was forbidden in his presence. In early adulthood he married a beautiful princess and had a son.

But as destiny would have it, despite these elaborate precautions, Buddha came upon a sick person, an old man, and a corpse. These sights altered the entire landscape of his mind. "What gives me true pleasure?" he wondered. "I know pleasures are fleeting, and I know the price I am paying to enjoy them. I also know I will be deeply disappointed when these pleasurable objects are no longer available, or when my own body and senses are no longer fit to enjoy them. But what I do not know is the source of pain and sorrow, their cause, or their cure. I must discover the cause of sorrow and uproot it forever."

With this resolve, Buddha left the palace. He committed himself to intense study, which led him to believe the path of renunciation would reveal the true nature—as well as the cause and the cure—of sorrow and pain. He firmly believed that the practice of austerity would burn his inner impurities, allowing the mind's brilliance to come forward.

At the peak of his practice of austerity, he sat under a bodhi tree without eating, drinking, or sleeping. On the forty-ninth day, when he was only semiconscious and on the verge of death, a woman named Sujata slipped some water into his mouth and made him take a spoonful of rice pudding. Buddha regained consciousness. He recognized that austerity had weakened his body, crippled his senses, and dulled his consciousness. He realized his consciousness and energy had returned soon after he had taken a sip of water and a bite of rice pudding. This caused him to redefine and redesign his practice.

Buddha concluded that extremes lead nowhere. He decided the middle path is the right path. Neither indulgence nor rigid restraints are conducive to self-discovery. In the light of this new understanding, Buddha began his meditation practice again. He ate neither too much nor too little; he slept neither too much nor too little; he exercised moderately. He interacted with people in moderation. Unlike before, his practice did not numb his senses. He had plenty of energy to meditate and enough energy to sustain the normal functions of his senses. He made no effort either to indulge his senses or to restrain them. This effortless effort allowed him to focus his mind on the object of meditation without fear of his unknown and unpredictable mental tendencies.

Samadhi, the highest state of meditation in yoga, is divided into two broad categories: lower and higher, with a period of transition between the two. This is the transition from duality to non-duality, from meditation on an object to meditation without an object. This transitional stage is lit by *prajna*, the light of inner intelligence. In this stage, the yogi is fully aware of the phenomenal world, which is ruled by time, space, and the law of cause and effect, as well as the realm that transcends it. In simple language, the yogi is simultaneously "here" and "there." In this state, the practitioner is able to witness his strengths and weaknesses and his positive and negative tendencies. By using the power of inner intelligence, the yogi is able to distinguish uplifting tendencies from afflicting ones and eventually transcend both.

When Buddha reached this transitional state, he found himself surrounded by Mara, sensual craving fueled by lust, and Mara's vast army of cravings. Buddha made no effort either to welcome them or to ward them off. He remained still. As an observer he saw the dynamics of his unfulfilled desires. In the light of prajna, inner intelligence, he saw how trivial those cravings are and how exhausting it is to fulfill them. He saw that fulfillment of one craving gives birth to yet another level of craving. He saw how cravings entangle individuals in the cycle of samsara. Buddha decided the path constructed and sustained by cravings was not his path. Thus he dismissed the world run by cravings and entered higher samadhi, a state marked by absolute peace and wisdom.

•••• ••• • •••••

Buddha and Narada are not the only seekers confronted with distracting and disturbing thoughts. All of us have a wealth of such thoughts. But these masters were much more vigilant than we are. They made a concerted effort to go all the way to the source of their disturbing thoughts. They were not afraid of discovering the worst in themselves. They had cultivated the wisdom to see, compare, and contrast their positive and negative tendencies. They had also cultivated the capacity to look at both from an equal distance. They had the courage to disidentify with the tendencies they found hindering their practice. All these qualities helped these souls protect and nurture their technique-driven and contemplative practices.

The Practice of Purashcharana

The traditional system of meditation places equal emphasis on the technique-driven component of meditation and on the set of practices that allow us to recognize and conquer the mental tendencies that hinder our quest. When put into practice in a well-structured, time-bound way, this twofold dimension of meditation is technically known as *purashcharana*. Because of its inherent design, this well-structured, time-bound meditation forces us to transcend our limitations and take a step (*charana*) forward (*purash*), and continue moving forward until the practice is complete.

We often do our daily meditation by rote. We take our seat, do some preparatory practices, and begin meditating. During our meditation, random thoughts continually appear and disappear. As long as these random thoughts do not completely block the flow of meditation, we tell ourselves we are meditating. Because the time we allot for meditation is quite short and filled with preparatory and ancillary practices, we do not reach a place where our meditation is hijacked by the mind's hidden contents. This fills us with the pseudosatisfaction of completing our daily 30-minute meditation. But this type of daily meditation fails to show us the true nature of our mind and its hidden contents. It has a calming effect on our body and nervous system, but contributes little to our self-realization. Only when we commit ourselves to a well-structured, time-bound practice with built-in contemplative tools do we get a chance to see, confront, and conquer the hidden contents of our mind. This allows meditation to bear optimal fruit.

The following experience shared with me by my teacher, Swami Rama, is an example of a well-structured, time-bound practice with built-in contemplative tools. This story will also help us see how cleverly negative tendencies emerge, how they dull our power of discernment, how they motivate us to act against ourselves, and ultimately, how we can free ourselves from such tendencies once and for all.

Swami Rama, whom I always refer to as Swamiji, took monastic vows in late adolescence and attended college as a monk. Monastic rules demanded that he keep his interactions with others to a minimum. He was not supposed to interact with women, especially not with single women his own age. The more he complied with monastic rules the more attention he drew. Fearing he might violate his vows, he developed a way of keeping some distance from others while living among them. He avoided embracing his friends, shaking hands, and making eye contact with women. This left him with only a few friends, and even with them he had little in common. When college was in session, he was occupied with his studies, and during summer vacations, he returned to his master in the Himalayas.

His master was a great adept with more than half a century of direct experience. He did not want his student to grow up as a hedgehog, which curls up into a ball when threatened. He made sure Swamiji would discover and confront the hidden tendencies of his mind and conquer them before they could create havoc, particularly in his meditation. To this end, he instructed Swamiji to undertake a 40-day meditation practice while following the rules of purashcharana. The place his master chose for the practice was near a cremation ground outside Darjeeling, in the eastern Himalayas.

The practice Swamiji undertook there was not new in itself. He had been doing this practice for several years. What was new were the set of dos and don'ts and the contemplative disciplines accompanying the practice. As per his master's instructions, Swamiji lived in a small hut at the edge of a cremation ground. He cooked his meals and washed his clothes. With the exception of occasional trips to town to fetch groceries and firewood, he spent all his time in the immediate vicinity of the cremation ground.

As part of his practice, Swamiji woke up at dawn, bathed in the nearby stream, and sat for meditation. That took barely three hours. Cooking, eating, and doing dishes took another two hours. He was instructed to spend the rest of the time doing things we normally don't associate with meditation.

From sunrise to sunset Swamiji observed silence, which included refraining from reading and writing. The practice demanded that he go for a walk every afternoon. While walking he was instructed to pay attention to the beauty and grandeur of the mountains, discover his connection with them, and reflect on the purpose of their existence: Who are their parents? Who are their friends? What makes them so stable? What is their purpose? Why does each peak stand alone? How do they relate to the valleys? How do they feel when they are covered with snow and how do they feel when the snow melts away?

Swamiji was further instructed to sit on the stream bank and watch the constant flow of water, its dance with rocks and pebbles: What is its source? Does it know where it is going? Look at the flowers: What is the secret of their happiness? Are they aware they will soon drop their petals and become part of the dust? Do they care about the future that awaits them?

At night he was to contemplate the infinitely vast congregation of stars: Who is their creator? What sustains their existence? What are they trying to achieve by shining there? What is their contribution to the universe? Do these celestial bodies go through old age, disease, and death just as we do?

He was also instructed to watch what was going on at the cremation ground: How long has it been there? How many bodies has it consumed? Will its hunger ever be satisfied? Is anyone beyond its reach? What can I learn from the flames of the funeral pyres, which consume bodies so fearlessly?

His master instructed Swamiji to eat his meals only after offering them to divine providence. He told him to maintain the awareness that the food he ate during the forty days of the practice was meant for propitiating consciousness, which in her own mysterious way provides nourishment to the body and mind. When going to bed, he must offer his gratitude to Ratri Devi, the goddess of night, who skillfully takes our worries away, thus granting us sleep. Upon awakening, he must remember *chiti shakti*, the power of consciousness, who motivates our mind and heart to start our day and attend our dharma.

In concluding his instructions, his master said, "Never underestimate the power of simplicity. See how simple breathing is. You inhale and exhale. Such a simple phenomenon keeps you alive. When something goes wrong in your breath and you struggle to breathe, you realize its importance. The same is true with meditation. You understand the value of these simple-seeming practices only when you are in trouble."

Swamiji began his practice exactly the way his master had instructed. For the first few weeks, he enjoyed it immensely. Then he began missing his friends. He wanted to write to them and not having access to pen and paper made him restless. The more he remembered the instructions not to read or write, the more his restlessness grew. While taking his afternoon walk, he wanted to talk to the people working in the fields, but the practice demanded that he preserve his solitude and talk to the mountains instead. The more he craved human contact, the less he enjoyed the flowing streams, smiling flowers, and twinkling stars. He found no meaning in the funeral pyres. He still did his meditation, but the contemplative aspect of the practice declined drastically.

His master had told Swamiji that this forty-day practice would give him a direct experience of an aspect of himself he had never known before. Swamiji interpreted his master's prediction to mean he would have knowledge of his past life or what was going to happen in the near future. Or perhaps it meant he would know how many lifetimes he had been on the spiritual path. Or he would know his relationship with the sages of the tradition and see how much knowledge he had already amassed. . . . And all that knowledge would again come forward as the result of the practice.

During the last few days of the practice, Swamiji started counting the hours he spent in meditation. During the contemplative periods of the practice, he began re-evaluating his interpretation of his master's prediction and wondering if he was any closer to achieving what his master had promised.

On the thirty-ninth day, a train of thought began running through his mind during his afternoon walk: "How absurd it is that I'm talking to mountains. What is so spiritual about discovering my connection with them? Am I doing anything more than just killing time? My friends must be enjoying their summer vacation and here I am, practicing simplicity in the pursuit of discovering an aspect of myself previously unknown to me. If a thirty-nine-day practice has not yielded a result, why should I expect one more day to make any difference?"

Swamiji made a decision—he would stop his practice immediately, spend a few days in Darjeeling, and then return to Delhi. He picked up his belongings and walked toward the city. Passing through a street on the outskirts, he heard a song wafting from one of the houses. He found the chorus mesmerizing: "The night is long, and there is very little oil in the lamp. . . . Life is short, and the journey is long." The beat of the accompanying drum said, *dhik, dhik*, "shame on you, shame on you." Swamiji took it as a message, returned to his hut, and continued his practice.

On the fortieth day, he had the experience his master had predicted. During the last few moments of the practice, his sense of identity as an individual evaporated. His consciousness expanded beyond the boundaries of his body and conscious mind. Mountains, streams, stars, sky, the cremation ground—all merged in him and he merged in them. His expanded consciousness was neither small nor big, neither deep nor shallow. It contained neither past nor future, virtue nor vice. It was neither celestial nor earthly. It was free from any trace of bondage or freedom. It was an awareness that expressed the feeling of existence and non-existence simultaneously. This experience lasted a second or an eon—impossible to say, for it was outside the realm of time. The experience revealed an immutable truth: I am a child of immortality. So is everyone.

•••••••••••

These well-structured, time-bound practices illuminate the unlit corners of our mind, enabling us to see and experience contents unknown to us before. At the age of three, Swami Rama was adopted by his master, Bengali Baba. He grew up among sadhus who practiced austerity and had no material possessions. Even before he took vows of renunciation, Swamiji was cut off from family ties. The monastic environment prevented him from realizing he craved affection. When school was in session, he busied himself with his studies. During vacations, he was surrounded by his monastic family and occupied with his practices. Thus he never had the chance to see that the human in him was lonely.

During this forty-day practice, had he resorted only to a technique-driven practice of meditation, and had that practice been accompanied by the hardship of intense austerities, he could have completed it. But such a practice would not have given him an opportunity to see an aspect of himself that could be seen only with a clear, calm, energetic, and discerning mind.

On the surface, it appears that Swamiji's main problem was that he doubted the validity and efficacy of the practice. But it was deeper than that. Far outside his conscious awareness, he was caught between wanting and not wanting. His normal human nature wanted to give and receive love and affection. The monastic environment demanded he stay away from such worldly experiences. The pressures of monastic life enabled him to master the art of denial, but denial could not alter the truth.

The inherent nature of the contemplative aspect of the practice lifted the veil he had wrapped around himself over time. The combined forces of technique-driven practice and well-structured contemplation brought the light of his inner intelligence forward. He became aware of the truth he had been denying. He had enough courage and insight to transcend his denial, but he did not have enough courage and insight to acknowledge and embrace the newly revealed reality. That is what caused him to quit the practice on the thirty-ninth day. But as soon as he heard the song and the accompanying drum, he was charged with both the wisdom and the strength to embrace this new reality, though he realized he would be able to do so only by completing the practice.

Some of us are endowed with a high degree of sincerity and mental clarity. We know we can achieve our goal through uninterrupted, sustained practice. We also know what makes a practice perfect and truly rewarding. But what we do not know is that we fear the immersive nature of the practice. We want to experience our unbound, undying, all-consuming consciousness but not at the expense of losing our self-identity. Sincerity, burning desire, and clarity in our practice transport us to the state of unconditional peace and joy, but as soon as the process of becoming one with peace and joy commences, we become frightened. Instead of trustfully embracing it, we flee. To illustrate this, I will share an experience of my *gurubhai*, one of Swamiji's senior students.

•••••••••••••

My gurubhai was born and raised in a distinguished family of scholars. As a teenager, he memorized the Vedas, Upanishads, and other ancient scriptures. He received his higher education in Europe and became an associate professor at the University of Minnesota. But his academic career was only a small slice of his life. He was also a sincere seeker.

As more of his time and energy was consumed by family duties and professional responsibilities, his desire for the spiritual quest intensified. During summer vacations he traveled to India in search of a competent master, but he always returned disappointed. As destiny would have it, he eventually met Swami Rama of the Himalayas right there in Minneapolis.

When he met Swamiji, the first thought that flashed through his mind was, "Perhaps I'm wasting my time. Why would a Himalayan adept come to America?" The only thing that impressed him was that Swamiji was a former Shankaracharya, the most prestigious religious post in Hinduism. But this impression was soon undermined by the simplicity of the meditative technique Swamiji taught him. The contemplative principles were the most unimpressive part of the practice because, according to my gurubhai, they were completely lacking philosophical, metaphysical, or spiritual depth. The Shankaracharya factor, however, made him stick to the practice.

Three years went by. My gurubhai continued his practice with the occasional complaint that he was not seeing a result.

Then the frequency of these complaints began to increase. Swamiji reminded him to pay attention to his deep-rooted negative tendencies, and to fear in particular. My gurubhai denied outright that he had any fear. Hearing this, Swamiji designed a well-structured, time-bound practice with contemplative principles built in.

My gurubhai began his purashcharana practice in the basement of his home. He cleaned the space and lit a flame as instructed. Except when he was teaching his classes at the university, he observed silence. The time not spent in meditation was occupied with simple stretching, breathing exercises, and contemplation. In relation to food and sleep, he followed the rhythm of nature. As time passed, his practice deepened and became more refined. He was grateful to Swamiji for teaching him and glad he was taking time to do the practice.

One day toward the end of his practice he slipped into an extremely joyful state. Initially he was aware of the joy that was pulling him deeper, but eventually, as this awareness deepened, his sense of self-identity as a meditator faded and he was immersed in all-consuming joy. The cognition of time and space vanished. Then suddenly a thought flashed: "How long have I been in this state?"

This brought his sense of self-identity back to the forefront of his mind. Even though he was still experiencing inner joy, its all-consuming nature had evaporated. He felt an urge to look at the clock, but the urge to recapture the immersive state of inner joy kept his eyes closed. When the clash between these two opposing impulses became unmanageable, he was forced to open his eyes.

He looked at the clock and saw he had been meditating for

four and a half hours. He was thrilled at his accomplishment until he realized he had missed the class he was supposed to be teaching. The mind game began. He thought, "Well, I've already missed the class, so let me go back to my meditation."

He closed his eyes, but a few minutes later, long before he could touch the immersive state of inner joy, another thought surfaced: "If I keep falling into this joyful state every time I meditate, how am I going to teach at the university? How am I going to take care of my family and myself? I wish I had some other means of meeting my needs so that I could meditate without such worries." At some point, this train of thought became irresistible and he stopped trying to meditate.

Several years later, while sharing this experience with me, my gurubhai said, "Pandit Rajmaniji, since then I have been meditating several hours a day. Each day I pray to reach that immersive state of inner joy. Lately I have chosen to sit in the early hours of the morning when it's completely quiet. Yet I rarely reach that state, and even when I do, it doesn't last very long."

I asked him, "During that first overwhelming experience, what was the source of your curiosity about how long you had been meditating? Did the curiosity come first and cause you to fall from that immersive state, or did the fall from that state come first, making room for the curiosity to emerge?"

"It's hard to say," he replied. "As I reflect, it becomes clear that the root cause of both the curiosity and the falling from the immersive state is fear. What I do not understand is fear of what?"

This dialogue between the two of us took place at the Himalayan Institute in Pennsylvania at a time when our teacher, Swami Rama, was in residence. When the opportunity arose, my gurubhai asked him, "Swamiji, I know fear is my biggest obstacle, but

I do not know what I'm afraid of. I know very well that nothing is a greater achievement than freedom from fear, and I also know this freedom comes from meditation. When meditation is just about to give me a firsthand taste of this freedom, why do I run from it?"

"Fear of losing one's self-identity is the greatest of all fears," Swamiji said. "You are afraid of losing your identity. Like most people in the world, you are a complicated person. You are a scholar and you are a spiritual seeker. The scholar in you craves distinction. The spiritual seeker in you craves equality. The craving for distinction is constantly searching for honor. The craving for equality is constantly searching for love and humility. These two opposing cravings are a major part of your self-identity.

"Craving for distinction is a threat to your humility, and humility is a threat to your desire for distinction. You have an intellect sharp enough to know that you are full of fear, but your intellect is not pure enough to discover the exact nature and source of your fear. You are not aware of the fact that on one hand you desire to be free, but on the other hand you do not want to let go of the part of your self-identity that binds you to the superficial reality of honor, glamour, and recognition.

"Meditation by nature engenders simplicity. Simplicity nullifies complexity. During meditation, when your complex nature is being replaced by simplicity, you become frightened. Attachment to the complex ingredients of the mind forces you to run away from a state of consciousness that is straightforward and all-inclusive. Losing the familiar world of your self-identity to the unfamiliar world of all-pervading, universal consciousness is unacceptable to you. You overcome this subtle and potent ignorance through the repeated practice of purashcharana."

Undertaking a Purashcharana

Doubt, loneliness, and fear are only a few of the subtle tendencies that drain the vitality of our body and cloud the brilliance of our mind. The practice of purashcharana enables us to discover the sources of those tendencies and heal the injuries they have caused to our body and mind. As described earlier, *purashcharana* means "a step to move forward." In most systems of meditation, the concept of purashcharana does not exist, and even when it does, it simply means completing a certain number of mantra recitations within a specific period of time. In the school of Vishoka Meditation, purashcharana is well defined.

The general guidelines for undertaking a purashcharana require avoiding all extremes. For example, the place where you practice should be clean, not too bright, not too dark, not isolated but not near a crowded place. It should be neither noisy nor dead silent. It should be free from strong aromas, both pleasant and unpleasant. It should be neither overly decorated nor completely bare. Similarly, during the purashcharana, you should neither actively seek engagement in worldly matters nor totally shield yourself. In other words, staying in the middle ground fulfills the first general requirement for undertaking a purashcharana.

Always begin your practice with a formal statement of your *sankalpa*, the intention behind your practice. Do this methodically. For example, after you are seated, formally declare, "Today, on {date} at {place}, as part of my {9-day-long, 40-day-long, etc.} purashcharana, I {name} resolve to meditate. May this meditation practice infuse my mind with clarity and stability and my heart with purity, love, and compassion. May the forces of creation, the sages of the tradition, and the enlightened masters, who always seek out those stranded on the path, witness my resolution and shower their blessings for a successful meditation." Recite this sankalpa mentally, or say it out loud if it will not disturb others.

Meditate three times a day. Repeat your sankalpa before each session. If your mind begins to entertain random thoughts, making it hard for you to meditate, pause for a few moments and remind yourself that you have resolved to complete this purashcharana. Have a short dialogue with your mind: "Mind, you have been attending such thoughts for ages. After the purashcharana is over, you will have plenty of time to embrace such thoughts again. Can't you spare just 30 minutes for meditation and see how much peace and happiness you gain from it?" Do not prolong this dialogue. With this gentle yet emphatic reminder, return to your meditation.

At the end of each meditation session offer the fruits of the practice to the forces that led you to complete it successfully. Just as you made a formal declaration of your intention before beginning your practice, now offer the fruits of the practice with a formal declaration: "Due to the innate quality of the building blocks of my body, senses, and mind, or due to habits and strong impressions of the past, I may not have attended my meditation in as deep and pristine a manner as my inner being intended, and yet, I pray to the forces governing our inner and outer worlds to accept the fruits of my practice as a pure and unblemished offering."

Adherence to these general guidelines builds a strong foundation for undertaking specific forms of purashcharana. Specific purashcharanas are advanced in terms of both intensity and complexity. They are designed in the light of our physical capacity, emotional maturity, intellectual clarity, and most important, the precise goal of the practice. If you are well versed in the philosophy and metaphysics behind your system of meditation, you can design an intensive course of purashcharana on your own. In this case, it is highly advisable that you consult authoritative scriptures pertaining to the practice and follow the guidelines strictly. If you are not fully confident about your understanding, consult a qualified teacher.

Commitment to an advanced purashcharana assumes you have been practicing meditation for a while and have already completed at least one purashcharana following the general guidelines. That will have given you a good understanding of your strengths and weaknesses. You will have identified the most stubborn obstacle blocking your path and will have been trying your best to overcome it. This is where an advanced purashcharana comes in.

A few examples of how to design an advanced course of purashcharana to overcome specific obstacles will give you an idea of what is involved.

Overcoming Sloth and Inertia

Intellectually you understand the importance of meditation in attaining inner peace and happiness, but you are struggling with your deeply ingrained habit of sloth and inertia. You have difficulty getting out of bed in the morning. When you do get up, it takes awhile before you feel fresh and energetic enough to do your meditation.

What you do not realize is that your body and mind are still wrapped in laziness and yet you are forcing yourself to sit for meditation anyway. As part of your system of meditation you declare to yourself and the forces of the cosmos, "Today, at such-and-such time and such-and-such place, I am going to meditate." In the first few minutes, you experience your breath becoming smooth and your mind calming. Ten minutes later, however, you start to feel drowsy and soon fall asleep. This has been a consistent pattern. To overcome this problem, commit yourself to a 10-day advanced practice of purashcharana.

In this case, dietary disciplines, cleansing techniques, and relaxation and breathing practices are central. Start your purashcharana with a detoxification that emphasizes cleaning your GI tract. During the course of your purashcharana, eat light meals, drink plenty of water, and evacuate your system shortly after you wake up in the morning. Cleanliness of the digestive system and clarity of mind go hand in hand. Do not indulge in vigorous exercises, including too much asana. Walking twice a day, doing some simple yoga stretches followed by deep relaxation and alternate nostril breathing will help you overcome your laziness. Go to bed on time and employ willpower to wake up on time. Before going to bed, practice sandbag breathing for five minutes, followed by alternate nostril breathing.

Meditate 30 minutes in the morning right after you have evacuated your system and bathed; meditate 30 minutes before lunch; and meditate another 30 minutes before dinner. In between, do your walking, stretching, breathing, and relaxation. Reading an inspiring text, keeping the company of like-minded people, refraining from gossip, and avoiding political and sectarian discussions are important parts of the practice.

Within a few days, your body will begin to obey the commands of your mind. Without much effort, you will wake up at the same time every morning and have a regular bowel movement upon waking. Your body will become lighter and your mind fresher. Obstacles arising from sloth and inertia will fade.

In the week or so remaining in your purashcharana, your

meditation will create mental grooves deep enough to motivate you to meditate regularly. Furthermore, during this 10-day practice, you will slip into a highly refined immersive state of meditation more than once. The memory of the joy arising from that immersive state will become your inner guide, and you will look forward to reaching that state again and again.

Overcoming Low Energy

In another instance, you might be suffering from low energy. You are mentally alert, yet you feel physically exhausted. In this case, in addition to following all the guidelines in the above example, add a unique element to your meditation.

While in meditation, bring your attention to your navel center and visualize an image of fire. The flames naturally tend to move upward and form a triangular shape. Flames are never static—they always move. The pelvic bowl serves as the base of this triangle of fire. The tip of the flames is touching your sternum. Thus your entire tummy from pelvis to sternum is encased in fire. The navel is at the center of this fire.

If you are suffering from poor digestion and a weak immune system, you will find it somewhat difficult to visualize the fire, and so you may want to have a picture of fire in front of you. If you decide to use the picture of fire as a tool, place the picture six to eight feet away, at eye level. Keep your meditation room dark and illuminate only the picture.

When I was practicing this, I used a night-light with a cover on three sides, which I painted black. I placed the light facing the picture of the fire, which made the fire look vibrant—the room was slightly lit by the vibrancy emitted from the picture. Because nothing other than the image of the fire was in view, it was easy to hold that image in my mind. After finishing *samikarana pranayama*, I gazed at the image of the fire. When I realized the image had become stable in my mind, I closed my eyes and visualized that image at my navel center. This image was the focal point of my meditation. Whenever I felt the image fading, I opened my eyes, gazed at the image for a few seconds, and then again brought that image back to my navel center. Very soon I was able to meditate on fire at my navel center without gazing at the picture. You can do the same.

Banishing Disturbing Thoughts, Confusion, and Weak Memory

If you have been struggling with disturbing thoughts or have been suffering from confusion and indecisiveness, or if your retentive power is weak, meditate at the center of your forehead.

As we have seen, the practice of meditation invariably begins with *aharana pranayama*. Aharana pranayama is the foundation for samikarana pranayama, and samikarana pranayama evolves into vishoka. Vishoka has four distinct points of concentration: the opening of the nostrils, the inner corners of the eyes, the center between the eyebrows, and the center of the forehead. If you feel that finding a solution to disturbing thoughts, confusion, and a weak memory is what is most crucial to your inward journey, once you have reached the center of your forehead, stay there and meditate.

At the outset of each session, as part of your sankalpa, officially declare to yourself and the forces of the cosmos that you are undertaking your purashcharana with the intention of achieving this goal, and request the benevolent forces that fill the space inside and outside you to help you achieve it.

Calming Emotional Turmoil

If you are suffering from emotional turmoil, the best place to focus your mind during your purashcharana is the heart center. In this case, after completing samikarana pranayama, take five to seven breaths between the center of your forehead and the heart center. With each exhalation, descend to your heart, and with each inhalation, ascend from your heart to the center of your forehead. Each time you return from the forehead to your heart, bring the joyful feeling from the region of your forehead to your heart.

By the time you are taking your sixth or seventh breath, you will become oblivious of the physical dimension of the distance between your heart and forehead. You will be left with the feeling of a continuum, the center of which is your spiritual heart. At this stage, do not force yourself to become aware of the physical location of your heart. Wherever you feel the gravitational pull of joy, that particular point in the space of consciousness is your spiritual heart.

Mantra-Centered Purashcharanas

Mantra-centered purashcharanas are unique to our tradition. There are thousands of mantras. Some are documented in the scriptures and others are passed on through the oral tradition. A small number of mantras are for spiritual upliftment, but the majority are for overcoming obstacles that have their origin in our mind or in the world outside us. Obstacles arising from fear, grief, and suicidal tendencies, for example, are the domain of mantra-centered purashcharanas. Precautions and prerequisites for these purashcharanas are stricter than those that do not include mantras.

Mantras are not ordinary compositions, nor are they expressions of the intellect—they are revealed words, embodiments of divine grace, which descended on the horizon of consciousness of those completely immersed in the highest state of meditation. In this immersive state, the duality of the meditator and the object of meditation vanish, and intuitive power flows unhindered. The unconditional love and grace of the divine take audible form. That is how revealed mantras come into being.

From time to time, adepts in the tradition have received these revealed mantras from the primordial pool of divine providence. These adepts embraced and assimilated the shakti of these mantras with unalloyed love and conviction. Maintaining the purity of these mantras and passing them on to successive generations is an important part of the tradition's responsibility. When applied at the right time in the right manner, these mantras unveil their transformative power, just as they did for those to whom they were revealed.

The masters in our tradition do not associate these mantras with a particular language. If necessary, they will explain the meaning the way it flashed in the mind of the original adept, but the most important part of the practice is connecting one's consciousness with the consciousness of the adept and allowing this awareness to create an internal atmosphere conducive to the manifestation of the mantra's potency.

A purashcharana with mantra at its core is precise and methodical. In our current cultural climate in which spirituality is so closely identified with religion, and religious sentiments are so volatile, it is best to undertake a purashcharana of revealed mantras only after you have transcended the narrow concepts and precepts of religiosity and have understood the universality of the experiences of the adepts. You must cultivate the conviction that the immersive nature of meditation enabled the adepts to rise above the narrow notions of caste, creed, and ethnicity.

You must also understand that these adepts were perfect containers for receiving the love, knowledge, and power of divine providence, and were perfect conduits for this gift. This understanding will help you find your unique connection with them. Thereafter, you will be practicing the mantra through their mind and experiencing it through their heart. Unless you cultivate this quality, it is better to optimize your practice of meditation by committing yourself to practices that do not depend on mantras.

The Best Place to Practice

Regardless of whether you are engaging in a general or in a specific purashcharana, the energy of the place where you do your practice plays a significant role. There are places so charged with transformative power that as soon as you enter them, the scattered forces of your mind spontaneously begin to align themselves with the inherent quality of that space. In our tradition, such a space is called a *tirtha*, shrine.

If the intensity of the energy of a shrine is strong enough, it will subdue and even nullify the negative tendencies of your mind and awaken the tender and innocent qualities of your heart. Your outwardly running mind will turn inward. This spontaneous inward flow of your mind empowers you to find your inner connection. Once you are connected to your inner being, the quality of your practice increases exponentially. Practicing a purashcharana in the space encompassed by the energy field of a shrine fulfills most of the prerequisites and lifts many of the conditions and injunctions that apply to a normal course of practice. To benefit fully from a purashcharana at a shrine, all you have to do is come with an open and flexible mind.

The energetically vibrant space of the shrine opens the door to your own inner shrine. In the peaceful space of your inner shrine you discover your connection with your core being. Once you find this inner connection, disturbances arising from worldly relationships lose their grip on your mind. When you experience your inner connection during each meditation session, your relationship with your core being intensifies until it becomes a living reality. It now has the capacity to ward off the negative tendencies arising from deep-rooted, afflicting karmic impressions. You are able to meditate more effortlessly and efficiently.

Reaching the Source of Joy

Bear in mind that none of the tools, means, techniques, or ancillary and advanced practices described in these pages are as effective and potent as the constant awareness of the undeniable truth: life is short and the journey is long. We must look and see what we have accomplished in the past and what we are trying to achieve now. Have any of our achievements brought us closer to our inner self? Will any of these achievements go with us when we leave this world? The sap of life is decreasing with each passing day, yet we waste our time grieving over the past and worrying about the future. The present is the only time we have to discover the best in ourselves and the best in the world, and it is being eaten up by past and future concerns. We must learn to live in the present and to live fully. This is what yogis call practicing constant awareness. This awareness nourishes our meditation.

In an attempt to help us optimize the practice of meditation, masters in the past have prescribed hundreds of formulas. All of those formulas have come from their own direct experiences, and yet none fully serve our needs. The seekers who came before us complained that their meditation wasn't bearing the fruit they expected, and the seekers in the present have similar complaints. Addressing this perennial problem, the great sage Vyasa states in his commentary on the *Yoga Sutra*, "One can experience meditation [yoga] only through practice. Meditation is the cause of meditation. One who is not negligent in the practice of meditation reaches the immersive state of meditation" (YS 3:6).

No formula will work if we do not meditate, and any valid formula will work if we do. Among all the tools, means, and enablers, nothing is more effective than reflecting on another undeniable truth: once we conquer the roaming tendencies of our mind and restore our equanimity, we have conquered the whole world. This conquest is the fruit of meditation.

If we understand that this priceless victory is the outcome of our meditation, we will be willing to go to great lengths to achieve it. Our conscience will refuse to count hours, days, months, or years. The joy of attending our practice will pull us forward. We will not trivialize the grandeur of our practice by measuring it with the yardsticks of stress reduction or changes in our brain waves, although these benefits will come as by-products of our meditation. When we embrace meditation to rediscover and restore the pure and pristine nature of our mind, our negative mental tendencies will automatically weaken and the obstacles arising from them will fade away.

The value we place on meditation is an integral part of the

practice. The goal we aspire to gives a concrete shape to our meditation. The clearer our understanding of the relationship between meditation and the restoration of our inner equanimity, the more joyfully and enthusiastically we will attend our meditation. A joy-driven meditation leads us all the way to the place within us where we will find the cure for all our pain and sorrow.

APPENDICES

The Vishoka Meditation Practice

Sit in a comfortable meditative pose with your head, neck, and trunk aligned. Withdraw your mind from all directions, and become aware of your body and the space it occupies.

Aharana Pranayama

1. Take 5–7 deep, smooth breaths.

2. Bring your attention to the center of your forehead and take 3 deep, relaxed breaths.

3. Take 1 deep, complete breath at each of these points:
    o Center between the eyebrows
    o Eyes
    o Nostrils
    o Throat
    o Shoulders
    o Upper arms
    o Elbows
    o Wrists
    o Palms

4. Bring your attention to your fingertips and take 2 complete breaths.

5. Take 1 complete breath at the:
   o Palms
   o Wrists
   o Elbows
   o Upper arms
   o Shoulders
   o Throat
   o Heart
   o Bottom of the sternum
   o Navel center
   o Pelvis

6. Take 2 complete breaths at the perineum.

7. Take 1 complete breath at the:
   o Pelvis
   o Navel center
   o Bottom of the sternum
   o Heart
   o Throat
   o Nostrils
   o Eyes
   o Eyebrow center
   o Center of the forehead

8. Finally, bring your attention to your crown center and take 3 breaths.

9. Finish your final breath with an inhalation and seamlessly slide into the next step of the practice.

Samikarana Pranayama

1. As you exhale, feel the combined forces of your mind and breath descending from your crown and sweeping through the:
    o   Forehead
    o   Eyebrow center
    o   Nostrils
    o   Throat center
    o   Heart center
    o   Bottom of the sternum
    o   Navel center
    o   Pelvis
    o   Down to the perineum

2. Upon completing your full exhalation, without pausing, begin inhaling and feel your breath flowing upward through the:
    o   Pelvis
    o   Navel center
    o   Bottom of the sternum
    o   Heart center
    o   Throat center
    o   Nostrils
    o   Eyebrow center
    o   Center of the forehead
    o   All the way to the crown, as you complete a full inhalation

3. Repeat 10 times. The 10th breath completes samikarana pranayama

Vishoka Meditation
(main body, comprised of 4 steps)

Samikarana ends with an inhalation up to the crown center.

1. Without pausing, begin exhaling down through the:
   o Forehead
   o Center between the eyebrows
   o Nostrils
   o And into the space extending 6–9 inches from the opening of your nostrils (zero point)

   The zero point is the space corresponding to the furthest frontier from the opening of your nostrils, where you retain an energetic awareness of your breath.

2. Begin your inhalation at the zero point. Continue inhaling gently and smoothly while the breath:
   o Passes through the space in front of your face
   o Enters the nostrils
   o Travels through the inner corners of the eyes
   o Travels through the center between the eyebrows
   o Reaches all the way to the center of the forehead

3. Without pausing, begin exhaling and descend through the:
   o Center between the eyebrows
   o Inner corners of the eyes
   o Nostrils
   o Back to the zero point

4. Without pausing, begin inhaling from the zero point all the way to the center of your forehead, and descend again as you exhale.

5. Repeat 3–5 times.

Step I: Awareness at the opening of the nostrils

1. Bring your attention to the opening of the nostrils.

2. Begin inhaling from the zero point and pass through the space in front of your face.

3. Allow your mind to register the instant your breath touches the opening of your nostrils and becomes charged with the joy of stillness unique to this spot.

4. Continue inhaling, moving up through the:
   - o Nasal passage
   - o Inner corners of the eyes
   - o Center between the eyebrows
   - o To the center of the forehead

5. Without pausing, begin exhaling, letting the united forces of your breath and mind move through the:
   - o Center between the eyebrows
   - o Inner corners of the eyes
   - o Nasal passage
   - o Opening of the nostrils
   - o Back to the zero point

6. Repeat 3–5 times.

Step II: Awareness at the inner corners of the eyes

1. Begin inhaling from the zero point.
   o Pass through the space in front of your face.
   o Feel the touch of the incoming breath at the opening of your nostrils.
   o Travel through the nasal passage.
   o Pass through the area of the inner corners of the eyes, noting the feeling of sweetness unique to this spot.

   Continue inhaling:
   o Through the center between the eyebrows
   o To the center of the forehead

2. Without pausing, exhale as the united forces of your breath and mind move through the:
   o Center between the eyebrows
   o Inner corners of the eyes
   o Nasal passage
   o Opening of the nostrils
   o Back to the zero point

3. Repeat 3–5 times.

Step III: Awareness at the eyebrow center

1. Now keep the center between the eyebrows as your focal point.

2. Begin inhaling at the zero point. Pass through the:
   o   Space in front of your face
   o   Opening of the nostrils
   o   Nasal passage
   o   Inner corners of the eyes

3. Pass through the eyebrow center and be aware of the upward-moving energy that is unique to this space. Allow it to spontaneously pull your awareness toward the center of the forehead.

4. Continue inhaling to the center of the forehead.

5. Without pausing, exhale as the united forces of your breath and mind move through the:
   o   Center between the eyebrows
   o   Inner corners of the eyes
   o   Nasal passage
   o   Opening of the nostrils
   o   Back to the zero point

6. Repeat 3–5 times.

Step IV: Awareness at the center of the forehead (ajna chakra)

The distinctive quality of the ajna chakra is inner light and intuitive power. This final step of Vishoka Meditation brings the unique energies of all the previous steps to a point of focus at the ajna chakra.

1. Begin inhaling at the zero point. Letting the mind flow along with the breath, pass through the:
   o Space in front of your face
   o Opening of the nostrils
   o Nasal passage
   o Inner corners of the eyes
   o Eyebrow center
   o To the center of the forehead

2. Without pausing, exhale as the united forces of breath and mind pass through the:
   o Center between the eyebrows
   o Inner corners of the eyes
   o Nasal passage
   o Opening of the nostrils
   o Back to the zero point

3. Feel your breath as a wave of awareness moving up and down in this pranically charged energy field. This wave is the pulsation of pure consciousness. You are this wave and this wave is you.

4. Your goal is to eventually stay with step IV for 9–10 minutes.

Preparatory Practices

The 75-Breath Practice

This practice is centered around a series of sweeping breaths that accompany your awareness from point to point through your body. An upward flowing awareness accompanies each inhalation, and a downward flowing awareness accompanies each exhalation. As soon as your inhalation reaches its natural completion, you reach your upward destination point, the crown of the head, and begin exhaling to reach your next downward destination point. As you travel from point to point, be aware of the key points (ankles, knees, perineum, navel, heart, throat, forehead) through which you pass on the way to or from your crown.

Throughout the entirety of this practice, there should be a seamless flow of breath, with no pause between inhalation and exhalation or between exhalation and inhalation.

1. Enter *shavasana* (corpse pose) by lying flat on your back on a firm surface, legs naturally spread apart, arms a comfortable distance away from your body, palms up, with your fingers slightly curled. Support your head and neck with a thin pillow, and cover yourself with a light blanket if you desire.

2. Feel the space your body occupies and the unique self-awareness filling that space.

3. Take a few complete breaths and establish an energetic awareness of the space your body occupies, from crown to toes.

4. Bring your awareness to your toes to begin.

5. Inhale from toes to crown and exhale from crown back to toes 10 times. Remember not to pause between inhalation and exhalation or between exhalation and inhalation. On the 10th exhalation, do not exhale all the way to the toes, but only to the ankles, and begin inhaling from there.

6. Inhale from ankles to crown and exhale from crown to ankles 10 times.

7. Inhale from each of the following points to the crown and exhale back again 5 times:
   o Knees
   o Perineum
   o Navel
   o Heart
   o Throat
   o Center of the forehead (On the last exhalation, exhale from the crown to the opening of the nostrils.)

8. Inhale from the opening of the nostrils to the center of the forehead and exhale from the center of the forehead to the opening of the nostrils 25 times.

9. Release your awareness of inhalation and exhalation to or from any point, and experience the space your body occupies. Feel each breath as a pulsation of prana from within this space.

10. When you are ready to conclude, deepen your breath to bring your awareness outward. Bring some small movements into your fingers and toes. Roll over onto your left side before coming upright into a seated posture.

11. Take a few breaths and gently open your eyes. If you are going to practice meditation after the 75-breath practice, be sure to sit up before you begin your meditation.

Crocodile Pose

The crocodile pose is one of the best ways to restore the rhythmic movement of the diaphragm. The weight of the torso compresses the abdomen while allowing the diaphragm to move up and down freely.

1. Lie on your abdomen with your legs about shoulder width apart and your toes turned outward.

2. Fold your arms and rest your forehead on your forearms or the backs of your hands.

3. Breathe as deeply and fully as possible.

4. As you inhale, observe how your abdomen presses against the floor while simultaneously expanding upward and sideways.

5. As you exhale, observe how your abdominal region relaxes, allowing the entire abdomen to flatten against the floor.

6. Take 10 breaths in this manner.

Sandbag Breathing

One of the easiest and most efficient ways of strengthening the diaphragm and abdominal region is to breathe with a weight on the abdomen. Begin with a 5-pound bag of sand malleable enough to mold itself to the shape of your stomach, and work your way up to 10–16 pounds of weight. Make sure the sandbag is not resting on any portion of your ribcage.

1. Lie on your back in *shavasana* (corpse pose) and take a few breaths. Take note of how your breath flows before you put the sandbag on.

2. Place the sandbag on your abdomen.

3. Relax and breathe. Enjoy breathing into the resistance.

4. Notice that the inhalation requires some effort, but during the exhalation the weight pushes your abdomen down, allowing you to expel air from your lungs effortlessly.

5. Increase the weight only when the urge to lengthen your exhalation indicates that your diaphragm is becoming stronger.

6. Work with this practice for 5–7 minutes and then remove the sandbag. Enjoy a few breaths without the sandbag before completing the practice.

Nadi Shodhana

The practice of *nadi shodhana* (channel purification) balances the energetic potential of our subtle energy channels, or nadis, by weaving a balanced sequence of inhalations and exhalations through each nostril in an alternating pattern. Our practice will consist of two rounds separated by a complete breath.

1. Find a stable, comfortable, seated posture so that your head, neck, and spine are aligned in a neutral position.

2. Breathe naturally and cultivate a smooth, deep, diaphragmatic breath.

3. Take a few complete breaths and allow your inhalation and exhalation to be balanced and of even duration.

4. Bring your attention to the touch of breath at your nostrils.

5. Begin your first round by inhaling through both nostrils, and then use your fingers to:
    o   Close your left nostril and exhale through the right nostril
    o   Close your right nostril and inhale through the left nostril
    o   Exhale through the right
    o   Inhale through the left
    o   Exhale through the right

o   Inhale through the right

o   Exhale through the left
o   Inhale through the right
o   Exhale through the left
o   Inhale through the right
o   Exhale through the left

o   Inhale through the left

o   Exhale through the right
o   Inhale through the left
o   Exhale through the right
o   Inhale through the left
o   Exhale through the right

6.   Release the fingers, then inhale evenly through both nostrils. Feel the smoothness and subtlety of your breath now.

7.   For the second round, reverse the orientation so that you begin with the opposite side. This balances the two sides, left and right, of the nervous system and prepares you to enjoy a deeper state of inward awareness in meditation.

8. Begin your second round by inhaling through both nostrils, and then use your fingers to:
   o Close your right nostril and exhale through the left
   o Close your left nostril and inhale through the right
   o Exhale through the left
   o Inhale through the right
   o Exhale through the left

   o Inhale through the left

   o Exhale through the right
   o Inhale through the left
   o Exhale through the right
   o Inhale through the left
   o Exhale through the right

   o Inhale through the right

   o Exhale through the left
   o Inhale through the right
   o Exhale through the left
   o Inhale through the right
   o Exhale through the left

9. Release your hand from your nostrils and then breathe smoothly and evenly through both nostrils.

10. Enjoy the uniquely balanced state of awareness after this practice, and the natural inward flow of your mind, perhaps toward the center of your forehead.

11. If you wish to prolong your practice of nadi shodhana, do another two or four rounds in the same fashion (i.e., an even number of rounds), so that you maintain the same number of inhalations and exhalations through both nostrils. Gently open your eyes to conclude the practice.

So Hum Pranayama

So hum pranayama (also referred to as *shvasa-prashvasa pravahi*) means "a technique that allows the inhalation and exhalation to flow seamlessly." This calming pranayama helps to eliminate the pause between breaths by mentally synchronizing inhalation and exhalation to the silent awareness of the sound *so hum.*

1. Sit in a comfortable posture with your eyes closed and withdraw your mind from all worldly objects and concerns.

2. Become aware of your body and the space it occupies and mentally draw a circle of light around yourself.

3. Feel your own presence in the region of your forehead. Take a couple of breaths and let this feeling of self-presence fill the space in front of your face and all around your head.

4. Take 3 relaxed breaths, feeling the touch of cool air at the opening of your nostrils as you inhale and the touch of warm air as you exhale.

5. Recall the sound *so hum* silently.

6. As you inhale, listen to the sound *so.* As you exhale, listen to the sound *hum. So* and your inhalation and *hum* and your exhalation are a single stream of awareness. *Hum* begins at the tail end of *so,* and *so* begins at the tail end of *hum.*

7. The sound *so hum* and the breath become an inseparable stream of awareness, and this awareness begins to flow seamlessly.

8. Continue your practice for about 5 minutes.

About the Author

Spiritual head and chairman of the Himalayan Institute, Pandit Rajmani Tigunait, PhD, is the successor of Swami Rama of the Himalayas. Lecturing and teaching worldwide for nearly 40 years, he is the author of 17 books, including his latest, *Vishoka Meditation: The Yoga of Inner Radiance*, and groundbreaking commentaries on the *Yoga Sutra* of Patanjali—*The Secret of the Yoga Sutra: Samadhi Pada* and *The Practice of the Yoga Sutra: Sadhana Pada*. He is a regular contributor to the Himalayan Institute's online Wisdom Library, the driving force of the Institute's global humanitarian projects, and the visionary behind the Institute's newly consecrated Sri Vidya Shrine in Honesdale, Pennsylvania.

Pandit Tigunait holds two doctorates: one in Sanskrit from the University of Allahabad in India, and another in Oriental studies from the University of Pennsylvania. Family tradition gave Pandit Tigunait access to a vast range of spiritual wisdom preserved in both the written and oral traditions. Before meeting his master, Pandit Tigunait studied Sanskrit, the language of the ancient scriptures of India, as well as the languages of the Buddhist, Jaina, and Zoroastrian traditions. In 1976, Swami Rama ordained Pandit Tigunait into the 5,000-year-old lineage of the Himalayan Masters.

HIMALAYAN INSTITUTE®

The main building of the Himalayan Institute headquarters near Honesdale, Pennsylvania

The Himalayan Institute

A leader in the field of yoga, meditation, spirituality, and holistic health, the Himalayan Institute is a nonprofit international organization dedicated to serving humanity through educational, spiritual, and humanitarian programs. The mission of the Himalayan Institute is to inspire, educate, and empower all those who seek to experience their full potential.

Founded in 1971 by Swami Rama of the Himalayas, the Himalayan Institute and its varied activities and programs exemplify the spiritual heritage of mankind that unites East and West, spirituality and science, ancient wisdom and modern technology.

Our international headquarters is located on a beautiful 400-acre campus in the rolling hills of the Pocono Mountains of northeastern Pennsylvania. Our spiritually vibrant community and peaceful setting provide the perfect atmosphere for seminars and retreats, residential programs, and holistic health services. Students from all over the world join us to attend diverse programs on subjects such as hatha yoga, meditation, stress reduction, ayurveda, and yoga and tantra philosophy.

In addition, the Himalayan Institute draws on roots in the yoga tradition to serve our members and community through the following programs, services, and products:

Mission Programs

The essence of the Himalayan Institute's teaching mission flows from the timeless message of the Himalayan Masters, and is echoed in our on-site mission programming. Their message is to first become aware of the reality within ourselves, and then to build a bridge between our inner and outer worlds.

Our mission programs express a rich body of experiential wisdom and are offered year-round. They include seminars, retreats, and professional certifications that bring you the best of an authentic yoga tradition, addressed to a modern audience. Join us on campus for our Mission Programs to find wisdom from the heart of the yoga tradition, guidance for authentic practice, and food for your soul.

Wisdom Library and Mission Membership

The Himalayan Institute online Wisdom Library curates the essential teachings of the living Himalayan Tradition. This offering is a unique counterpart to our in-person Mission Programs, empowering students by providing online learning resources to enrich their study and practice outside the classroom.

Our Wisdom Library features multimedia blog content, livestreams, podcasts, downloadable practice resources, digital courses, and an interactive Seeker's Forum. These teachings capture our Mission Faculty's decades of study, practice, and teaching experience, featuring new content as well as the timeless teachings of Swami Rama and Pandit Rajmani Tigunait.

We invite seekers and students of the Himalayan Tradition to become a Himalayan Institute Mission Member, which grants unlimited access to the Wisdom Library. Mission Membership offers a way for you to support our shared commitment to service, while deepening your study and practice in the living Himalayan Tradition.

Spiritual Excursions

Since 1972, the Himalayan Institute has been organizing pilgrimages for spiritual seekers from around the world. Our spiritual excursions follow the traditional pilgrimage routes where adepts of the Himalayas lived and practiced. For thousands of years, pilgrimage has been an essential part of yoga sadhana, offering spiritual seekers the opportunity to experience the transformative power of living shrines of the Himalayan Tradition.

Global Humanitarian Projects

The Himalayan Institute's humanitarian mission is yoga in action—offering spiritually grounded healing and transformation to the world. Our humanitarian projects serve impoverished communities in India, Mexico, and Cameroon through rural empowerment and environmental regeneration. By putting yoga philosophy into practice, our programs are empowering communities globally with the knowledge and tools needed for a lasting social transformation at the grassroots level.

Publications

The Himalayan Institute publishes over 60 titles on yoga, philosophy, spirituality, science, ayurveda, and holistic health. These include the best-selling books *Living with the Himalayan Masters* and *The Science of Breath*, by Swami Rama; *The Power of Mantra and the Mystery of Initiation, From Death to Birth, Tantra Unveiled*, and two commentaries on the *Yoga Sutra—The Secret of the Yoga Sutra: Samadhi Pada* and *The Practice of the Yoga Sutra: Sadhana Pada—* by Pandit Rajmani Tigunait, PhD; and the award-winning *Yoga: Mastering the Basics* by Sandra Anderson and Rolf Sovik, PsyD. These books are for everyone: the interested reader, the spiritual novice, and the experienced practitioner.

PureRejuv Wellness Center

For over 40 years, the PureRejuv Wellness Center has fulfilled part of the Institute's mission to promote healthy and sustainable lifestyles. PureRejuv combines Eastern philosophy and Western medicine in an integrated approach to holistic health—nurturing balance and healing at home and at work. We offer the opportunity to find healing and renewal through on-site wellness retreats and individual wellness services, including therapeutic massage and bodywork, yoga therapy, ayurveda, biofeedback, natural medicine, and one-on-one consultations with our integrative medical staff.

Total Health Products

The Himalayan Institute, the developer of the original Neti Pot, manufactures a health line specializing in traditional and modern ayurvedic supplements and body care. We are dedicated to holistic and natural living by providing products using non-GMO components, petroleum-free biodegrading plastics, and eco-friendly packaging that has the least impact on the environment. Part of every purchase supports our Global Humanitarian projects, further developing and reinforcing our core mission of spirituality in action.

For further information about our programs, humanitarian projects, and products:

call: 800.822.4547
e-mail: info@HimalayanInstitute.org
write: The Himalayan Institute
952 Bethany Turnpike
Honesdale, PA 18431
or visit: HimalayanInstitute.org

We are grateful to our members for their passion and commitment to share our mission with the world. Become a Mission Member and inherit the wisdom of a living tradition.

HIMALAYAN INSTITUTE®

inherit the wisdom of a living tradition today!

As a Mission Member, you will gain exclusive access to our online Wisdom Library. The Wisdom Library includes monthly livestream workshops, digital practicums and eCourses, monthly podcasts with Himalayan Institute Mission Faculty, and multimedia practice resources.

Mission Membership Benefits

Wisdom Library

Netra Tantra: Harnessing Healing Force (Part 1)
Pandit Rajmani Tigunait, PhD | September 28, 2017
Read more

- **Never-before-seen content from Swami Rama & Pandit Tigunait**
- **New content announcements & weekly blog roundup**
- **Unlimited access to online yoga classes and meditation classes**
- **Members only digital workshops and monthly livestreams**
- **Downloadable practice resources and Prayers of the Tradition**

Get FREE access to the Wisdom Library for 30 days!

Mission Membership is an invitation to put your spiritual values into action by supporting our shared commitment to service while deepening your study and practice in the living Himalayan Tradition.

BECOME A MISSION MEMBER AT:
himalayaninstitute.org/mission-membership/

The Secret of the Yoga Sutra
Samadhi Pada
Pandit Rajmani Tigunait, PhD

The Yoga Sutra is the living source wisdom of the yoga tradition, and is as relevant today as it was 2,200 years ago when it was codified by the sage Patanjali. Using this ancient yogic text as a guide, we can unlock the hidden power of yoga, and experience the promise of yoga in our lives. By applying its living wisdom in our practice, we can achieve the purpose of life: lasting fulfillment and ultimate freedom.

Paperback, 6" x 9", 331 pages
$24.95, ISBN 978-0-89389-277-7

The Practice of the Yoga Sutra
Sadhana Pada
Pandit Rajmani Tigunait, PhD

In Pandit Tigunait's practitioner-oriented commentary series, we see this ancient text through the filter of scholarly understanding and experiential knowledge gained through decades of advanced yogic practices. Through *The Secret of the Yoga Sutra* and *The Practice of the Yoga Sutra*, we receive the gift of living wisdom he received from the masters of the Himalayan Tradition, leading us to lasting happiness.

Paperback, 6" x 9", 389 Pages
$24.95, ISBN 978-0-89389-279-1

800-822-4547
shop@HimalayanInstitute.org
HimalayanInstitute.org

HIMALAYAN
INSTITUTE·

VISHOKA MEDITATION

The Yoga of Inner Radiance

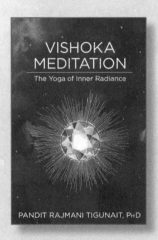

Imagine a life free from pain, sorrow, and negativity and infused with joy and tranquility. The ancient yogis called this state vishoka and insisted that we all can achieve it. The key is a precise set of meditative techniques designed to unite mind and breath and turn them inward, allowing us to heal and rejuvenate ourselves on every level of our being.

In *Vishoka Meditation: The Yoga of Inner Radiance*, Pandit Tigunait makes meditation as practiced by the ancient yoga masters accessible to a modern audience, offering step-by-step instructions to guide us to this illumined state of consciousness. Grounded in the authentic wisdom of a living tradition, the simple—yet profound—practice of Vishoka Meditation is the perfect complement to your existing yoga practice, as well as a powerful stand-alone meditation practice.

800-822-4547
shop@HimalayanInstitute.org
HimalayanInstitute.org

HIMALAYAN INSTITUTE

VISHOKA MEDITATION

The Yoga of Inner Radiance

Grounded in the authentic wisdom of a living tradition, the simple—yet profound—practice of Vishoka Meditation is the perfect complement to your existing yoga practice, as well as a powerful stand-alone meditation practice.

Learn Vishoka Meditation® Today!

- In-person Vishoka Meditation workshops at the Himalayan Institute and locations worldwide

- Online Vishoka Meditation webinars

- Vishoka Meditation teacher training certification program

- Vishoka Meditation immersion retreats, in-person and online

www.vishokameditation.org

Touched by Fire
Pandit Rajmani Tigunait, PhD

This vivid autobiography of a remarkable spiritual leader—Pandit Rajmani Tigunait, PhD—reveals his experiences and encounters with numerous teachers, sages, and his master, the late Swami Rama of the Himalayas. His well-told journey is filled with years of disciplined study and the struggle to master the lessons and skills passed to him. *Touched by Fire* brings Western culture a glimpse of Eastern philosophies in a clear, understandable fashion, and provides numerous photographs showing a part of the world many will never see for themselves.

Paperback with flaps, 6" x 9", 296 pages
$16.95, ISBN 978-0-89389-239-5

At the Eleventh Hour
Pandit Rajmani Tigunait, PhD

This book is more than the biography of a great sage—it is a revelation of the many astonishing accomplishments Swami Rama achieved in his life. These pages serve as a guide to the more esoteric and advanced practices of yoga and tantra not commonly taught or understood in the West. And they bring you to holy places in India, revealing why these sacred sites are important and how to go about visiting them. The wisdom in these stories penetrates beyond the power of words.

Paperback with flaps, 6" x 9", 448 pages
$18.95, ISBN 978-0-89389-211-1

800-822-4547
shop@HimalayanInstitute.org
HimalayanInstitute.org

HIMALAYAN INSTITUTE®

Meditation and Its Practice
Swami Rama

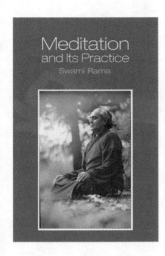

In this practical guide to inner life, Swami Rama teaches us how to slip away from the mental turbulence of our ordinary thought processes into an infinite reservoir of consciousness. This clear, concise meditation manual provides systematic guidance in the techniques of meditation - a powerful tool for transforming our lives and increasing our experience of peace, joy, creativity, and inner tranquility.

**Paperback, 6" x 9", 128 pages
$12.95, ISBN 978-0-89389-153-4**

The Art of Joyful Living
Swami Rama

In *The Art of Joyful Living*, Swami Rama imparts a message of inspiration and optimism: that you are responsible for making your life happy and emanating that happiness to others. This book shows you how to maintain a joyful view of life even in difficult times.

It contains sections on transforming habit patterns, working with negative emotions, developing strength and willpower, developing intuition, spirituality in loving relationships, learning to be your own therapist, understanding the process of meditation, and more!

**Paperback, 6" x 9", 198 pages
$15.95, ISBN 978-0-89389-236-4**

800-822-4547
shop@HimalayanInstitute.org
HimalayanInstitute.org

HIMALAYAN
INSTITUTE·

Sri Sukta

Tantra of Inner Prosperity

Sri Sukta—a cluster of sixteen Vedic mantras dedicated to the Divine Mother—is one of the greatest gifts to humanity given to us by the ancient sages. These awakened mantras empower us to pull the forces of abundance and nurturance toward ourselves so we can experience life's fullness.

Sri Sukta: Tantra of Inner Prosperity is the modern practitioner's guide to these mantras. Pandit Rajmani Tigunait's beautiful translation, commentary, and delineation of the three stages of formal practice help us unravel the mystery of Sri Sukta. This volume offers a rare window into the highly guarded secrets of Sri Vidya tantra—the heart of a living tradition—and reveals the hidden power of these mantras.

The wisdom of Sri Sukta is needed now more than ever. It holds the key to our individual peace and prosperity, and to a collective consciousness healthy and rich enough to build an enlightened society.

800-822-4547
shop@HimalayanInstitute.org
HimalayanInstitute.org

HIMALAYAN
INSTITUTE®